Termites in the Trading System

The Council on Foreign Relations is an independent, nonpartisan membership organization, think tank, and publisher dedicated to being a resource for its members, government officials, business executives, journalists, educators and students, civic and religious leaders, and other interested citizens in order to help them better understand the world and the foreign policy choices facing the United States and other countries. Founded in 1921, the Council takes no institutional positions on matters of policy. The Council carries out its mission by maintaining a diverse membership; convening meetings; supporting a Studies Program that fosters independent research; publishing *Foreign Affairs*, the preeminent journal on international affairs and U.S. foreign policy; sponsoring Independent Task Forces; and providing up-to-date information and analysis about world events and American foreign policy on its website, CFR.org.

JAGDISH BHAGWATI

Termites in the Trading System

How Preferential Agreements Undermine Free Trade

A Council on Foreign Relations Book

OXFORD
UNIVERSITY PRESS

2008

OXFORD
UNIVERSITY PRESS

Oxford University Press, Inc., publishes works that further
Oxford University's objective of excellence
in research, scholarship, and education.

Oxford   New York
Auckland   Cape Town   Dar es Salaam   Hong Kong   Karachi
Kuala Lumpur   Madrid   Melbourne   Mexico City   Nairobi
New Delhi   Shanghai   Taipei   Toronto

With offices in
Argentina   Austria   Brazil   Chile   Czech Republic   France   Greece
Guatemala   Hungary   Italy   Japan   Poland   Portugal   Singapore
South Korea   Switzerland   Thailand   Turkey   Ukraine   Vietnam

Copyright © 2008 by Oxford University Press, Inc.

Published by Oxford University Press, Inc.
198 Madison Avenue, New York, NY 10016

www.oup.com

Oxford is a registered trademark of Oxford University Press

Library of Congress Cataloging-in-Publication Data
Bhagwati, Jagdish N., 1934–
Termites in the trading system : how preferential agreements
undermine free trade / Jagdish Bhagwati.
p. cm.
Includes bibliographical references and index.
ISBN 978-0-19-533165-3
1. Tariff preferences.   2. Trade blocs.   3. Free trade.
4. Commercial policy.   5. International trade.
I. Title: Preferential agreements undermine free trade.   II. Title.
HF1721.B43 2008   382'.71—dc22   2007052420

9 8 7 6 5 4 3 2 1

Printed in the United States of America
on acid-free paper

In memory of Gottfried Haberler
A great international economist
and multilateralist

Every additional PTA [preferential trade agreement] will become one more obstacle to the universal and non-discriminatory trade liberalization that the world needs. PTAs have been more easily hijacked by special interest groups and are not resulting in really good instruments. . . . The present deals are little monsters that will be much regretted in the future.

—Ernesto Zedillo, former president of Mexico

In practice, bilateralism has fed off itself, intensifying the rush into preferential deals while draining energy from the Doha talks.

—Guy de Jonquières,
world trade correspondent, *Financial Times*

Contents

Preface

Few phenomena and institutions in international economics have attracted as much attention recently as the formation of free trade areas (FTAs), customs unions (CUs), and less comprehensive, partial preferential reductions of trade barriers. These phenomena are inherently discriminatory: they reduce trade barriers for members of the trade agreements but not for nonmembers. They therefore directly contradict the principle of nondiscrimination in trade that many economists and policy makers have traditionally valued as the sine qua non of sound trade policy and an essential cornerstone of the architecture of an efficient, even a fair, world trading system.

Why has this come about? Why have these preferential trade agreements (PTAs) proliferated in recent years, creating a systemic havoc in the world trading system?[1] What are the

1. I use the terminology of preferential trade agreements (PTAs) rather than the earlier one of regional trade agreements (RTAs) simply because the PTAs are not always regional in any meaningful sense. For example, the U.S.-Israel FTA is not regional. But the RTA terminology still persists at the WTO, which is not surprising since international bureaucratic and political usage often lags behind reality; G-77 now has many more than 77 developing country members, for example. Also, I do not use the terminology "bilaterals" because many PTAs are "plurilateral"—an infelicitous phrase that sounds like, and is, jargon—and consist of more than two, but less than all, nations as members.

consequences? Both the causes and consequences of this proliferation are complex and fascinating. Only recently have they
become the focus of serious inquiry from serious scholars of
international economics and from policy makers, who are both
in the middle of this pandemic. Acting like termites, PTAs are
eating away at the multilateral trading system relentlessly and
progressively. To use another analogy appropriate to what is
happening, the proliferating PTAs are leading us inexorably to
what might be aptly described as a trade wreck.

The growth of PTAs has itself led to serious scholarly breakthroughs in this branch of the welfare-theoretic analysis of
commercial policy, ranking just below the important revolu-
tion in the postwar theory of commercial policy constituted by
the welfare ranking of alternative policy interventions in the
presence of different market failures, domestic and foreign.[2]
I have participated actively in these developments,
starting with an early policy and conceptual treatment of
PTAs in the Harry Johnson Lecture in London (*The World
Trading System at Risk* [Princeton, N.J.: Princeton University Press, 1991]) and later in several books and professional journal articles that extended the theoretical analysis
in many directions. Many other distinguished economists
have also written on these issues, such as my frequent co-
author, Arvind Panagariya,[3] and my former students Richard

2. For a review of the scientific breakthroughs in commercial policy, which
have greatly strengthened the case for free trade, see chapter 1 of my Stockholm
School of Economics Lecture, *Free Trade Today* (Princeton, N.J.: Princeton
University Press, 2003).

3. I would highlight one joint essay in particular: Jagdish Bhagwati and
Arvind Panagariya, "Preferential Trading Areas and Multilateralism—Strangers,
Friends or Foes?" in Jagdish Bhagwati and Arvind Panagariya, eds., *The Economics
of Preferential Trade Agreements* (Washington, D.C.: American Enterprise Institute, 1996), chapter 1. Panagariya has been a prolific contributor to the theory
of PTAs on his own as well.

Brecher, Elias Dinopoulos, Jeffrey Frankel, Caroline Freund, Earl Grinols, Gene Grossman, Douglas Irwin, Pravin Krishna, Paul Krugman, Nuno Limao, and Devashish Mitra, all well-known economists by now.

I would also like to acknowledge the contributions over the past four decades of a number of other trade economists. Four among the older generation, no longer with us, deserve special mention: Gottfried Haberler (to whom this book is dedicated),[4] Harry Johnson, James Meade, and Jacob Viner. I would be remiss not to mention Kyle Bagwell, Richard Baldwin, Robert Baldwin, Claude Barfield, Eric Bond, John Chipman, Max Corden, Alan Deardorff, Christopher Dent, Peter Drysdale, Simon Evenett, Ross Garnaut, Koichi Hamada, Elhanan Helpman, Murray Kemp, Kala Krishna, Anne Krueger, Sajal Lahiri, Kelvin Lancaster, Robert Lawrence, Phil Levy, Richard Lipsey, Peter Lloyd, Michael Michaely, Robert Mundell, Martin Richardson, Ray Riezman, Gary Sampson, T. N. Srinivasan, Andre Sapir, Robert Stern, Robert Staiger, Lawrence Summers, Costas Syropoulos, Tony Venables, Henry Wan Jr., and Alan Winters. Indeed, the analysis of PTAs has attracted nearly all of the best economists working in the theory of international trade in the past half-century. I should also add that I have profited from reading the stout defense of multilateralism and acutely critical analyses of PTAs by the two leading economic journalists today, Clive Crook and Martin Wolf, both now at the *Financial Times*.

I have also been among the earliest economists to take to, and write with, distinguished trade lawyers. Chief among

---

4. Haberler, an economist of remarkable accomplishment, one of many famous émigrés from Austria to the United States, is rarely associated with the literature on preferential trade agreements. But he wrote on the subject, from a pro-multilateralist viewpoint, beginning in the 1940s and returned to the subject often.

those I have learned much from on the issues raised in this book is Robert Hudec, with whom I collaborated on important projects on the interface of economics and trade law and whose work on nondiscrimination is classic. I have also learned from my collaborator Petros Mavroidis, with whom I teach a joint course at Columbia Law School on World Trade Organization dispute settlement, which extends naturally to the WTO's Article 24 and other issues relevant to PTAs. I have profited from many conversations with Kenneth Dam, John Jackson, David Leebron, David Palmeter, and Merit Janow.

This short volume is not the place to look for theoretical breakthroughs. An extended treatment of the modern developments in the theoretical analyses can be found in the overview in the substantial volume edited by me, Pravin Krishna, and Arvind Panagariya, *Trading Blocs: Alternative Approaches to Analyzing Preferential Trade Agreements.*[5] The appendix here also provides a short and simple primer on the major developments in the scholarly work on PTAs that has literally transformed our understanding of PTAs in the postwar period.

My own writing on PTAs over more than two decades can be found in both professional journals and in several op-ed articles and essays in the *Economist,* the *Wall Street Journal,* and the *Financial Times.* In addition, I have given several lectures on the subject; among the latest was the Heinz Arndt Lecture at the Australian National University in 2007, where I recalled Arndt's brilliant historical analysis of how the 1930s witnessed the descent of the world trading system into protectionism and preferential trade agreements. Another was the keynote lecture to several CEOs in the Asian-

5. A more technical version is included in chapter 31 of the graduate textbook Bhagwati, Panagariya and Srinivasan, *Lectures on International Trade.*

Pacific Economic Cooperation region at Cebu in the Philippines. I urged them to oppose the idea, floated by some in the United States and presumably with the encouragement of the U.S. Trade Representative's Office, to create a free trade agreement of Asia and the Pacific, an idea that, though presented as providing a shot in the arm for the Doha Round, is in fact a shot in the head instead.

I have the unusual advantage of having thought about these matters deeply at the General Agreement on Tariffs and Trade (GATT) itself; few scholars at the frontier of science get this opportunity to get out of the ivory tower or have the inclination to use that opportunity. In 1991, Arthur Dunkel, who served for twelve years as the director general of the GATT, decided to create the special position of economic policy adviser to the director general and invited me to fill that position. Because I have a reputation for freely criticizing policies that I consider not to be in the public interest, and because I came from India to the United States, I asked him, "Whom did you clear my appointment with, India or the United States?" He said, "Neither, since both would have said no."

Dunkel talked to me a lot about the ongoing Uruguay Round, which was concluded soon after he was succeeded by Peter Sutherland, but I took the opportunity to urge him to have a special annual report on regionalism. Dunkel agreed, even though the matter was extremely delicate politically, given the European Union's embrace of PTAs and the sense that we were at the cusp of change in their direction. Indeed, the famous American economist Lester Thurow had already pronounced himself to be in that corner and was openly skeptical of multilateralism. He had famously announced at Davos, where the World Economic Forum meets, that GATT was dead.

Richard Blackhurst and Kym Anderson, the top economists at the GATT, worked on the project with me. It may interest those who criticize the WTO that, when I asked Dunkel for a small sum of money to have a conference where selected experts would explore some key issues that I felt were worthy of more intensive analysis for our report, he said he would have to work hard to get some money. He then came up with the princely sum of $25,000, and I persuaded some of the experts to use their frequent flyer miles to come on a pro bono basis to the conference, whose proceedings were published under the editorship of Anderson and Blackhurst. The cash-starved GATT then, and the WTO now, represent a special target of the militant antiglobalization nongovernmental organizations. But the irony is that the Bretton Woods institutions spend far more money (the travel budget alone of the International Monetary Fund exceeds the annual budget of the WTO) and are far less democratic in governance (the WTO works even today with consensus among members). Indeed, unlike the recent, virtual nominations of their own nationals by the United States and the European Union for the head of the World Bank and the IMF, respectively, the process that leads to selection of the director general of the WTO is totally democratic: the recent directors general, such as Supachai Panitchpakdi, Michael Moore, and Pascal Lamy, were fully examined on their views and experience for the job and had to work their way against serious candidates. Regardless, the report was virtually finished, but not issued, when Sutherland took over at the GATT and did not accept the suggestion from Dunkel that we finalize it for early release. Sutherland properly decided to concentrate instead on closing the Uruguay Round. The report was released only years later, after the Round was completed and the WTO was born in 1995.

When Supachai Panitchpakdi of Thailand, a Rotterdam PhD in economics and former deputy prime minister of Thailand, became the director general of the WTO in the footsteps of Michael Moore from New Zealand,[6] he formed an expert consultative group, of which I was a member and Sutherland was the chair. We returned to the question of PTAs in chapter 2 of the report we issued under the title *The Future of the WTO: Addressing Institutional Challenges in the New Millennium*. We carefully documented the harm that the proliferation of PTAs was causing to the multilateral trading system. This aspect of the report was widely highlighted in the media as its most important feature, and Sutherland focused on it in speeches at Davos and elsewhere.

These policy experiences (which also demonstrate how the GATT, and its successor, the WTO, have been cognizant at the highest levels of the systemic challenges posed by PTAs) and the serious scholarly contributions over many years have encouraged me to write this short book. I hope it will provide every scholar and policy maker with a comprehensive and analytically coherent, if brief, overview of the arguments that must be confronted if we are to cut

6. Michael Moore, not to be confused with his high-decibel namesake in the United States, had been the prime minister of New Zealand and had a respectable career that included work with the labor unions. He too had an external advisory group, of which the economists Robert Baldwin, Koichi Hamada, Sylvia Ostry, and I were members. He presided over the disruptions at the Seattle WTO meeting in November 1999 and was deeply distressed to see how uninformed emotions had triumphed over reasoned arguments at the time to kill the proposal to launch the first multilateral round of trade negotiations. Both that experience and his feistiness are evident in the following anecdote. He was being driven to a meeting in Australia when he encountered anti-WTO demonstrators who were chanting outrageously, "Michael Moore *kills* the Poor. Michael Moore *kills* the Poor." He asked his chauffeur to stop the car, got out, and confronted the demonstrators: "No, you are wrong: Michael Moore *eats* the Poor. Michael Moore *eats* the Poor." Befuddled, the demonstrators fell silent, recovering their wits and shouting their slogans again only after he had sped away. While I greatly admire what he did, and it was appropriate to the situation at hand, I have no talent in that direction and am content to demolish the populist arguments by using analysis, facts, satire, irony, and wit.

through the fog that surrounds this important and, in my view, pernicious development. How shall we return to the multilateralism that our trade policy makers have been extolling while their actions have been to undercut it? That is the ultimate issue that I deal with in this book. I argue that all is not lost and that we have remedial policies still open to us.

I would be remiss if I did not conclude by thanking Melanie Gervacio Lin, my remarkably gifted research associate at the Council on Foreign Relations during the year that I wrote this book. She had a highly theoretical training in international economics, which made her a splendid associate since PTAs raise profound theoretical issues. But she also took to the policy-related issues like a duck to water. Just as the Invisible Hand works wonders, Melanie's invisible input has transformed my book. I have also been helped immeasurably by her successors, Alex Noyes and Seth Flaxman. Alex helped me temporarily with the book until Seth came into Melanie's job. Seth has been a real delight to work with, with his remarkable energy, humor, and uncanny ability to track down obscure sources, cartoons, and portraits (especially of Joan Robinson, a great economist at Cambridge and one of my tutors; in the photograph Seth found, one sees a young woman, shy and gentle, before she had grown into her formidable stature). Ivan Crowley, one of my ablest students at Columbia University, has been a source of immense help as well. I must also acknowledge with gratitude the intellectual and research support provided to me by the Council on Foreign Relations, now under the able leadership of Richard Haass.

Jagdish Bhagwati
Council on Foreign Relations and
Columbia University
New York
December 2007

Termites in the Trading System

CHAPTER 1

Proliferating Preferential Trade Agreements

Most preferential trade agreements (PTAs) are in the form of free trade agreements (FTAs); a rare few contain an added common external tariff that converts them into customs unions (CUs).[1] As we contemplate their proliferation, it is useful to recall that the preferences in trade that they embody (whereby trade is freer for member countries than for nonmember countries) are not entirely new. Indeed, at critical times in history, trade preferences have been embraced with almost equal passion and have also attracted a

---

1. The glossary makes clear that preferences in the trading system arise in other ways, for example, the so-called one-way preferences granted under the GSP scheme, also explained there. Imperial preference was a PTA insofar as it permitted generally duty-free access by Britain to the markets of its colonies and dominions, while ensuring a moderately free reverse access by them to the British market, much the way several modern FTAs by superpowers such as the United States do in indirect ways when the other parties are weaker nations, as discussed in chapter 2.

strange, if fleeting, approbation from some of the finest minds among economists.[2]

KEYNES DURING WORLD WAR II

Perhaps the most striking historical flirtation with preferences in trade came from John Maynard Keynes, arguably the twentieth century's most influential economist. At the end of World War II, the British were skeptical of nondiscrimination as implied by the most favored nation (MFN) clause, which would automatically extend to every member country of the proposed trade institution the lowest tariff extended to any member. They also wished to hold on to their imperial preference, which extended British protection to its colonies and dominions. On the other hand, the Americans vigorously supported the MFN clause and favored nondiscrimination in the trading arrangements being contemplated after the conclusion of the war. They were led by Cordell Hull, the secretary of state from 1933 to 1944 and a recipient of the Nobel Prize for Peace; he believed, not without substance, that free trade would also lead to peace, not just prosperity. Keynes sided with his own, and made the following characteristically flamboyant statement: "My strong reaction against the word 'discrimination' is the result of my feeling so passionately that our hands must be free.... The word calls up and must call up ... all the old lumber,

2. Bilateral trade treaties go back centuries, of course; in the nature of the case, there was no "multilateral" trade initiative, though more than two countries were sometimes part of a trade treaty across countries under the same "empire." Pascal Lamy, in his interesting 2006 Gabriel Silver Memorial Lecture, "Multilateral and Bilateral Trade Agreements: Friends or Foes?," delivered at Columbia University on October 31, 2006, recalled the commercial treaty between the Egyptian pharaoh Amenophis IV and the king of Alasia during the fourteenth century BC, exempting Cypriot traders from customs duties in exchange for the importation of copper and wood.

most-favoured-nation clause and all the rest which was a notorious failure and made such a hash of the old world. We know also that it won't work. It is the clutch of the dead, or at least the moribund, hand."[3]

Yet once they had thought more deeply about the issue, Keynes and other British economists who were engaged in the negotiations with the United States that led to the final agreement in *Proposals for Expansion of World Trade and Employment* had come to accept the Cordell Hull view that nondiscrimination was a key principle that had to prevail in the proposed new regime for international trade.[4] Keynes, who thought that intellectual inflexibility was a mark of inferior minds,[5] then spoke in the House of Lords what are among his most eloquent words: "[The proposed policies] aim, above all, at the restoration of multilateral trade. . . . The basis of the policies before you is against bilateral barter and every kind of discriminatory practice. The separate blocs and all the friction and loss of friendship they must bring with them are expedients to which one may be driven in a hostile world where trade has ceased over wide areas to be cooperative and peaceful and where are forgotten the healthy

---

3. Quoted in Jay Culbert, "War-time Anglo-American Talks and the Making of the GATT," *World Economy*, 10, no. 4 (1987): 387. See the glossary for a brief description of the MFN clause.

4. The British negotiators finally did accept the principle of nondiscrimination but held on to imperial preference as a "grandfathered" exception.

5. Keynes vigorously defended the necessity of changing one's mind when reflection and experience so required. He has been credited with the remark "When the facts change, I change my mind. What do you do, sir?" Equally, he has been the butt of the teasing witticism, directed at economists generally, "When there are six economists, there are seven opinions, two being those of Keynes." At an after-dinner speech at the Yale Law School, I was subjected to a variant on this theme: "When there are six economists, there are six opinions," to which I offered the retort: "The matter is worse with lawyers. For every lawyer, there are six opinions if there are six clients."

Cordell Hull, President Franklin D. Roosevelt's secretary of state, won the Nobel Peace Prize in 1945. He worked to free trade from the ravages of protectionism wreaked by the Smoot-Hawley Tariff of 1930, being the architect of the Reciprocal Trade Agreements Act of 1934. He also was a fierce opponent of discrimination in trade. *Library of Congress, Washington, D.C.*

John Maynard Keynes, considered by many to be the greatest economist of the twentieth century, abandoned his embrace of preferences in trade and became an impassioned proponent of non-discriminatory, multilateral free trade. *John Maynard Keynes, Baron Keynes*, by Gwendolen ("Gwen") Raverat (née Darwin), pen and ink and watercolor, ca. 1908. *National Portrait Gallery, London.*

rules of mutual advantage and equal treatment. *But it is surely crazy to prefer that.*"[6]

THE 1930S DESCENT OF WORLD TRADE INTO PREFERENCES

As it happens, Keynes was reverting to an antidiscrimination view that had begun to make increasing sense to economists during the 1930s. World trade had gradually been shifting to a multilateral nondiscriminatory regime by growing acceptance of the MFN principle, under which any member of a trade treaty, later the GATT as well, would receive the same lowest tariff that any other signatory of the treaty would enjoy.[7] But world trade would soon turn disastrously to bilateralism and attendant preferences in trade.

Read almost any of the splendid accounts of world trade in the 1930s and you will find fulsome and fulminating accounts of how the tit-for-tat protectionism and the competitive depreciations of currency, which were intended to divert limited world demand to one's own goods to reinflate one's economy, led to extensive use of quotas, which are necessarily discriminatory unless auctioned off. They led also

---

6. Quoted in Culbert, "War-time Anglo-American Talks," 395, emphasis added; quoted in Bhagwati, *The World Trading System at Risk,* 64. Douglas Irwin has reminded me that, on the British scene, yet stronger proponents of nondiscrimination in trade were the economists Lionel Robbins and James Meade. See the account of the U.S.-British negotiations on the postwar trading architecture in Irwin, Mavroidis, and Sykes, *The Genesis of the GATT.*

7. As the glossary notes, there was the unconditional MFN, which is what I am describing. There was also the conditional MFN, under which the concessions made to one member of the treaty had to be offered to another member but did not automatically extend to that other member unless it made some reciprocal trade concessions as well. The GATT would embody the unconditional MFN as its central organizing principle, with some explicit exceptions, such as Article 24, which permitted the formation of FTAs and CUs.

to explicit bilateral treaties aimed at balancing trade flows bilaterally wherever possible.

British commercial policy began gloriously with Prime Minister Peel's unilateral embrace of free trade in 1846 and survived attempts at changing it to protectionism and bilateralism once Britain saw the emergence of Germany and the United States as a challenge to its trade hegemony. But the policy would be buried in the 1930s under the bilateral rubble. Thus, consider what the most accomplished analyst of the period, Heinz Arndt, had to say, in his Chatham House study, *The Economic Lessons of the Nineteen-Thirties,* about the decimation of nondiscriminatory free trade in Great Britain:

> One significant aspect of British commercial policy during the nineteen-thirties which stands out...was its general trend... towards increased state intervention and quantitative control. In this respect the adoption of protection was relatively unimportant.... The real breach...lay in the supersession of the free play of market forces by State control and diversion of foreign trade from its "natural" channels which was apparent in much of British commercial policy....By 1938 nearly half her total trade with foreign (non-Empire) countries was conducted under bilateral trade, payments or clearing agreements.[8]

8. Heinz W. Arndt, *The Economic Lessons of the Nineteen-Thirties* (London: Frank Cass, 1963), 118. Another important study at the time was *Commercial Policy in the Interwar Period: International Proposals and National Policies* (Geneva: League of Nations, 1942), chapter 8 in particular. For an acute, later account, see Charles P. Kindleberger, "Commercial Policy between the Wars," in P. Mathias and S. Pollard, eds., *The Cambridge Economic History of Europe,* Vol. 8 (Cambridge: Cambridge University Press, 1989), chapter 11, especially section 3 on "The Disintegration of World Trade."

Great Britain had been using the MFN clause as applicable to itself in its trade treaties, while occasionally extracting discriminatory treatment in its own favor from weaker nations, according to historians of the pre-1930s period. See Arndt, *Economic Lessons,* 119.

Heinz Arndt, a renowned Australian economist, emigrated from Europe to London, where he wrote his famous study of the world trading system in the interwar period at Chatham House, describing how the world had descended into protectionism and preferential trade in the 1930s.

It was manifest that protectionism, each trading nation acting on its own, had damaged the world trading system: each nation followed what the Cambridge economist Joan Robinson famously called "beggar my neighbour policies," and many were beggared in the end. By contrast, coordinated action, eschewing protection and agreeing to increase world aggregate demand (rather than seeking to divert to oneself a given, insufficient amount of world demand), would have produced a better result.

GATT: RESTORING PRIMACY TO NONDISCRIMINATORY FREE TRADE

The 1930s experience, and reflection on the descent of the world economy into bilateralism under policies of competitive tariff escalations and currency depreciations, provided the backdrop against which the architects of the postwar trading system were thinking of the design of the

Joan Robinson, a brilliant economist at Cambridge who was part of a remarkable group of economists around Keynes, wrote in 1937 about the uncoordinated resort in the 1930s to "beggar my neighbour" policies consisting of mutually nullifying competitive currency depreciations, advancing an argument that applied equally to the competitive raising of trade barriers that spread across the world after the 1930 Smoot-Hawley Tariff of the United States. Ramsey and Muspratt image, ca. 1932. *Lofty Images.*

new postwar trade architecture. However, the International Trade Organization (ITO) that was proposed as the "third" institution to go with the Bretton Woods institutions (the World Bank and the International Monetary Fund) was not even submitted for ratification by the U.S. Senate. In consequence, the General Agreement on Tariffs and Trade (GATT), which had been negotiated and signed in the interim with a view to its being incorporated within the broader ITO, became the de facto institution that would govern trade after 1948.

The GATT was designed to make uncoordinated free-for-all actions on raising trade barriers difficult through "rules" and "bindings" that would govern and discourage a lapse into competitive raising of trade barriers. Equally, it sought to resurrect multilateralism and assign a central role (via its key Article 1) to the restoration of the primacy of the MFN clause that would ensure nondiscrimination, an approach that the British finally accepted under American leadership (as exemplified by Keynes's conversion).

As it happens, the associated MFN-based multilateral reductions in trade barriers through multilateral trade negotiations (MTNs) worked wonders, reducing the trade barriers in manufactures in the rich countries to negligible levels today, after seven successive multilateral negotiations. (See Figure 1.1, which illustrates this enormous decline in tariff levels for the United States.)[9] The MTNs were known in common parlance as Rounds, prompting the witticism during the Uruguay Round that many unfamiliar with trade negotiations thought that this was a new Latin American dance. The primacy of MFN in the GATT's rules meant that any exceptions to MFN were *explicitly* provided for.

Unfortunately, such an exception was made via Article 24 for FTAs and CUs. Why? It seems from the historical record that few thought this exception would be used ex-

9. The reductions in trade barriers also came through unilateral liberalization, as documented and analyzed in Jagdish Bhagwati, ed., *Going Alone: The Case for Relaxed Reciprocity in Freeing Trade* (Cambridge, Mass.: MIT Press, 2002). That trade liberalization under GATT auspices has actually led to increased trade seems obvious, but has been contested by Andrew Rose, "Do We Really Know That the WTO Increases Trade?" *American Economic Review* 94, no. 1 (2004). However, his methodology fails to consider the counterfactual: What would have happened if there had been no GATT, with its rules and bindings and continued reduction of trade barriers? Is it not likely that postwar world trade would have collapsed into the 1930s type of free-for-all resort to protectionism as dictated by relatively unconstrained lobbies?

Index (Pre-Geneva Average Tariff = 100)

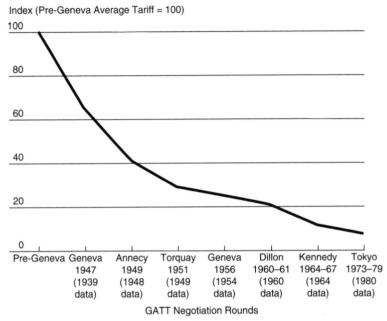

FIGURE 1.1. Successive GATT rounds and associated reductions in trade barriers (average U.S. tariff rates).

Note: Indexes are calculated from percentage reductions in average weighted tariff rates obtained from Michael Finger and the World Bank. The weighted average U.S. tariff rate after the Tokyo Round was 4.6 percent (World Bank 1987).

cept under rare circumstances, as it was thought that having to go the whole way toward virtually free trade and extending to nearly all commodities would discourage the resort to Article 24. It has been wittily remarked that this was like prohibiting lovemaking through promiscuity and sanctioning it only if the wedding rings were exchanged, a more demanding commitment.

Ironically, as I argue later, this option would be exercised by numerous members of the GATT, and now the WTO (which absorbed GATT in 1995). Even the disciplines imposed by Article 24 are no longer necessary under a new Enabling Clause if the preferential trade arrangement is exclusively among "developing country" members.[10]

THE PANDEMIC OF PTAS

There is yet another irony. The interwar proliferation of preferences was a result of an uncoordinated pursuit of protectionism, itself aided by the breakdown of financial stability and macroeconomic equilibrium in the world economy. But the current tide of preferences has been a result of politicians mistakenly, and in an uncoordinated fashion, pursuing free trade agreements because they think (erroneously) that they are pursuing a free trade agenda. I shall return to these themes in more depth in the next chapter.

So today we have a cumulative total of over 350 PTAs reported to the WTO (see Figure 1.2).[11] Even if only active PTAs are counted, the estimated total is still large (see Figure 1.3). By either count, the PTAs are evidently increasing continually.

Among economists, I was the earliest to warn against PTAs, starting in 1990 when I sensed that we were facing a systemic threat to the principle of nondiscrimination in

10. I discuss in chapter 2 how Article 24 was originally drafted to exempt customs unions but was then extended also to FTAs by the time the GATT articles were finalized. Because CUs are much more difficult to negotiate, since the common external tariff requires extensive negotiations and political commitment, the extension of Article 24 to include FTAs has also been a major contributory factor to their proliferation in recent decades.

11. This cumulative total exceeds those actually still active. At the same time, it does not include PTAs that have been formed but have not been notified, as required but with some latitude in timing. Also, the PTAs are under different articles of the GATT/WTO, as I discuss in chapter 2.

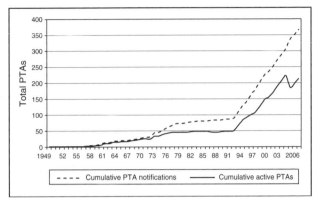

FIGURE 1.2. Cumulative PTAs notified to the GATT/
WTO (1949–2006).

Source: Roberto Florentino, Luis Verdeja, and Christelle
Tougeboeuf, World Trade Organization Secretariat, Trade
Policy Review Division, Geneva, 2007.

world trade.[12] I was then in a minority of one, even among
economists, many of whom thought I was a "multilateralist
freak." Arrayed on the other side were truly eminent
economists, among them Larry Summers, who became the
U.S. Treasury secretary, and the remarkable Paul Krugman,
my former MIT student and now *New York Times* columnist.

But now that the proliferation, and its many downsides
(which I document in chapter 3), has become evident, and
ever more threatening, I daresay that the profession has
moved like a herd into my corner. Pascal Lamy, currently
the director general of the WTO, once remarked that half

12. I raised the issue pointedly in my 1990 Harry Johnson Lecture in
London, published soon after as *The World Trading System at Risk*. As I write in
the preface, I also used my position as economic policy advisor to Arthur
Dunkel, the director general of the GATT, to get him to endorse PTAs, or
regionalism as they are misleadingly called at the GATT and now at the WTO,
as the subject of the GATT's special annual report.

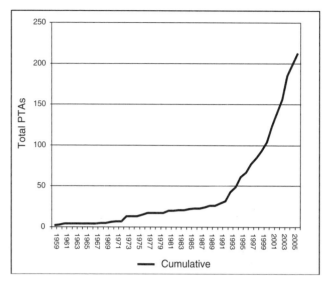

FIGURE 1.3. Cumulative active PTAs as notified to the GATT/WTO (1959–2005)

Source: Roberto Florentino, Luis Verdeja, and Christelle Tougeboeuf, World Trade Organization Secretariat, Trade Policy Review Division, Geneva, 2007.

the economists in the world were now opposed to PTAs. I retorted mischievously that this was an English understatement by a distinguished Frenchman; in fact, nearly all economists were opposed.

But almost all of the politicians have moved to the other corner. Faced with their imperviousness to reason, I thought I would try ridicule, the favored weapon of satirists and cartoonists. I noticed that there were proposals afoot to organize FTAs around oceans: in the Pacific there was the Pacific Free Trade Agreement, now called the Free Trade Area of Asia-Pacific; in the Atlantic we had the North Atlantic Free Trade Area, the real McCoy NAFTA, which actually had been embraced by many Atlanticists, including

Senator Jacob Javits, but had not come to pass. (Lesser FTAs have worked out and masquerade under that very acronym: the North American Free Trade Agreement among the United States, Canada, and Mexico, and the New Zealand–Australian Free Trade Agreement.) So I took out my daughter's map of the world, with rivers, bays, and lakes, and, in an article titled "The Watering of Trade,"[13] I made up a couple of funny FTAs built around such bodies of water. Imagine my surprise when I found that, by the time the article was published, these FTAs were already being discussed.

Then I discovered that the European Union, which started the pandemic while the United States had grossly aggravated it, applied its MFN tariff to only six countries—Australia, New Zealand, Canada, Japan, Taiwan, and the United States—with all other nations enjoying *more favorable* tariffs.[14] I asked Pascal Lamy, who was then the EU trade commissioner, Why not call it the LFN (least favored nation) tariff?

In short, we now have once again a world marred by discriminatory trade, much as we had in the 1930s, from which all sensible men and women had recoiled. How did this come about? What damage does it inflict on us? And what can we do about it?

13. Jagdish Bhagwati, "The Watering of Trade," *Journal of International Economics* 42, nos. 1–2 (1997): 239–41.

14. See Andre Sapir, "The Political Economy of EC Regionalism," *European Economic Review* 42 (1998): 717–32. Of course, these six countries include Japan and the United States, so if the share of total trade affected by tariff rates lower than the MFN tariff was the criterion used, the EU's current resort to discrimination would look less formidable. Nonreciprocal preferences extended to different groups of developing countries also account for the decimation of Europe's MFN tariff.

CHAPTER 2

Why Has the Pandemic Broken Out?

To understand the many reasons why PTAs have now turned into a pandemic and a pox on the world trading system, a phenomenon that could not possibly have been imagined by the architects of the GATT in their most fearful moments, it is necessary to first understand that few lay people and policy makers can appreciate the critical difference between PTAs and genuine multilateral, nondiscriminatory trade liberalization.

PTAS PIGGYBACKING ON SENTIMENT FOR FREE TRADE

As I argued in chapter 1, informed international economists were fully cognizant of the fact that PTAs represented a discriminatory phenomenon with a distasteful, indeed sordid, history. But this historical background, and the problems raised by discrimination in trade, were not part of the popular perception after World War II. The 1930s experience was far from the consciousness of the new generations who would influence policy making starting in the 1950s.

Many who vaguely understood that free trade was good, and the policy makers in the developed countries who were embracing the liberal international economic order (a precursor to the pro-globalization proponents of later years), saw *any* trade liberalization as good. If you were a free trader, you were supposed to be for all kinds of trade liberalization: any reduction of trade barriers was supposed to be as good as any other. It was as if an economist were to say, if you wish to cut spending in the national budget, just do it: every cut is as good as any other—a proposition that would soon be recognized as absurd. Somehow, the proponents of the prescription that one should liberalize in any way whatsoever manage to appear less foolish. So, in the public policy domain, the proponents of discriminatory reduction of trade barriers managed to piggyback, or ride free, on the proponents of multilateral nondiscriminatory free trade. And because the postwar period was characterized by extensive efforts at dismantling trade barriers, and MFN trade liberalization under GATT auspices went through successive rounds of multilateral trade negotiations (see Figure 1.1), the informed sentiment against FTAs and other PTAs became less compelling in the popular imagination.

And yet, while many lay people and politicians believed that even discriminatory lowering of trade barriers must surely be good as long as trade barriers were being dismantled, increasingly the sophisticated international economists realized that free trade areas (and other PTAs, such as customs unions, with a common external tariff) were a mix of free trade and protection. Why?

Because when a free trade area is formed and trade barriers are eliminated among members, that is, of course, freer trade. But if the external barriers by the member countries are left unchanged, then the handicap suffered by non-members in the markets of the member countries (vis-à-vis rivals producing in the member countries) increases. That constitutes increased protection. So FTAs are two-faced: they free trade among members, but they increase protection against nonmembers. This means they are fundamentally different from free trade. That is a subtle but important point (whose consequences are explored in the next chapter). We owe it to Jacob Viner, a great Canadian economist who taught at the University of Chicago and at Princeton. After the end of World War II he was asked by the Carnegie Endowment for International Peace to analyze the best international trade arrangements in the postwar period. He cautioned against assuming that what he loosely called customs unions were unambiguously welfare-enhancing.[1] In particular, because nonmembers were being discriminated against, he pointedly asked us to be alert to the fact that such discriminatory trade arrangements could divert trade from efficient, low-cost nonmembers to inefficient, higher cost member-country suppliers because the latter no longer had to pay the tariff duties that were still imposed on the former.

This critical difference between FTAs and genuine free trade eludes many untrained in international economics; unfortunately, the same must be said for many economists, who have no real knowledge of international economics. When the official midterm review of the North American Free Trade Agreement was undertaken in the United States,

---

1. The classic work in which Viner developed this critical message is *The Customs Union Issue*. The theoretical analysis that he developed, largely through arithmetical examples, relates to FTAs, where two member countries dismantle their trade barriers but do not undertake to devise a common external tariff, as required by a CU. That was also true of the flood of analytical literature that followed thereafter, with major contributions by the leading international economists of the period, including Harry Johnson and Richard Lipsey.

the prominent consulting firm Data Resources was given the job. It proceeded to analyze the effects of NAFTA by treating the preferential trade liberalization under the agreement as if it were MFN trade liberalization, missing the intrinsic nature of such PTAs. Indeed, as I argue in chapter 3, the lack of correlation between income expansion and trade expansion in Mexico in the decade after the formation of NAFTA, an unusual phenomenon since trade expansion is commonly associated with income expansion, may well have been due to the fact that trade expansion really consisted of trade diversion from North America at the expense of cheaper non-NAFTA suppliers.[2]

In fact, because many think that free trade areas and nondiscriminatory free trade are really the same, I have long argued that the FTAs, which constitute the overwhelming majority of the PTAs today (the only two major exceptions are the European Community and Mercosur in South America), should instead be called PTAs. That change would highlight the fact that the trade arrangements they constitute are preferential (i.e., discriminatory), whereas calling them FTAs lulls people into thinking that they are simply a species of free trade.

I once made this observation by remarking at a public lecture in Singapore some years ago that politicians, used to sound bites, could not read more than two words at a time. Thus, when they started reading "free trade agreements," they stopped after the first two words. Unfortunately, it turned out that there were some politicians in the audience.

---

2. I will argue there that, because the GATT bindings were higher than the applied tariffs, as is often the case everywhere, Mexico proceeded to raise its MFN tariffs, whereas the NAFTA tariff reduction schedule was tight, so the protectionist handicap of nonmember suppliers increased for two reasons due to the 1994 peso crisis interacting with NAFTA.

Fortunately, by now almost everyone uses the acronym PTAs; that battle has been won.

THE EASING OF GATT REQUIREMENTS TO CONCLUDE PTAS

It was not just the widespread intellectual failure to understand the critical distinction between freeing trade in discriminatory and nondiscriminatory ways that facilitated the spread of PTAs over time. The rot also set in because the relatively stringent requirements, originally built into Article 24 as preconditions that had to be satisfied before this exception to MFN could be utilized, were progressively reduced to near irrelevance. What was considered a relatively difficult exception to invoke before a PTA could be formed became an exception that became progressively easier to invoke, helping to turn a rivulet into a torrent. There are three principal ways this happened.

First, the specifics of the Article 24 exception to MFN were traceable to the negotiations over the proposed International Trade Organization, which was supposed to be the third institution alongside the IMF and the World Bank to oversee the world economy after World War II. But the ITO did not materialize.[3] It had originally been designed by the U.S. negotiators, who were the most forceful proponents of nondiscrimination in trade and the primacy of MFN in the postwar trade architecture, to extend only to customs unions. Thus, the exception to the MFN would be confined to PTAs that involved a common external tariff. This was clearly not an easy condition to fulfill.

3. The Havana Charter, which would have set up the ITO, failed to make progress in the U.S. Senate and was withdrawn by the Truman administration after the election in 1950.

But as the ITO negotiations progressed, the United States itself abandoned the customs union requirement and extended eligibility also to free trade areas that did not require an external tariff.[4] This abandonment has been traced by the political scientist Kerry Chase, who made an astonishing archival discovery. Apparently, the new position of the United States was not a result of changed intellectual convictions. Rather, it owed to expediency so as to accommodate a secret U.S.-Canada free trade agreement, which in the end did not transpire either.[5]

Alas, FTAs are far easier to agree to than CUs because they do not require difficult negotiations over a common external tariff. This is surely among the reasons why today we have two CUs—the European Community and Mercosur[6]—and a far larger and growing number of FTAs.

Second, the restrictive qualifications built into Article 24, whether for CUs or for FTAs, were often ignored. These restrictions were presumably intended both to minimize excessive resort to Article 24 and to ensure that nonmembers would not be subject to more discrimination than implied by the formation of the PTA itself. Similar restrictions have

4. As a result, the 1948 version of the Havana Charter for the ITO, in Article 44 of part IV on "Commercial Policy," explicitly included FTAs as a permissible exception to MFN. A comprehensive account of the transition to include FTAs (except for the subsequent discovery by Kerry Chase, cited in the next note) is provided in chapter 2 of John H. Mathis's important work, *Regional Trade Agreements in the GATT/WTO*. He also provides a helpful review (pp. 24–29) of the preferential arrangements in existence at the end of World War II, drawing on H. P. Widden, *Preferences and Discrimination in World Trade* (New York: Committee on International Policy, Carnegie Endowment for International Peace, 1945).

5. See Kerry A. Chase, "Multilateralism Compromised: The Mysterious Origins of GATT Article XXIV," *World Trade Review*, March 2006, 1–30.

6. Even then, the progress of Mercosur toward an effective CU has been halting, to say the least.

been built into Article 5 of the General Agreement on Trade in Services. (The acronym is GATS. It is rumored that "Trade" was added to the name because otherwise the acronym would have been GAS, recalling the way the UN Fund for Economic Development was handled: when the acronym was seen to be UNFED, they added "Special" so that the acronym would be SUNFED, reminding us of Sunkist oranges from Florida.) The GATS is one of the three legs—the other two being the original GATT and the agreement on "trade-related" intellectual property rights—on which the WTO, created at the end of the Uruguay Round, rests.

The main restrictive qualifiers that characterized Article 24 from the outset were as follows:

- An accepted plan, with a schedule, had to move the PTA from its initial formation to a full-fledged liberalization of trade within "a reasonable length of time" (paragraph 5). This would ensure that very long, undefined periods of "interim arrangements," during which the preferential reduction of trade barriers within the PTA would effectively turn it into less than 100 percent preferences of all kinds, were to be ruled out.[7]

- "Duties and other restrictive regulations on commerce" were (with specified exceptions permitted under GATT Articles 11, 12, 13, 14, and 20) to be "eliminated with respect to substantially all the trade between the constituent territories" (paragraph 8). Again, the intention was to rule out partial preferential reductions,

---

7. In strict theory, as developed particularly by the economist James Meade, one of the architects of the GATT, 100 percent discriminatory tariff reductions as in an FTA are not necessarily better than partial preferential reductions of trade barriers. But remember that the insistence on 100 percent tariff reduction was designed, almost certainly from a political economy viewpoint, to minimize the use of Article 24. The positive rationale for 100 percent preferences, on the other hand, is discussed in Bhagwati, *The World Trading System at Risk,* 64–66.

not through indefinite extension of the time during which "interim arrangements" would be in force, but through sectoral exemptions.

• Where the previous two provisions were aimed at ensuring that significant, partial tariff preferences were ruled out, there was also concern that any PTA not be used to raise trade barriers against others who were GATT members but not PTA members. Thus, as Viner pointedly noted, whereas a discriminatory PTA would inherently increase the handicap of nonmembers in the PTA's markets, Article 24 was designed to ensure that additional duties and restrictions would not be imposed on nonmembers that would exceed those obtaining prior to the formation of the PTA (paragraph 5).

In truth, however, such restrictions have been emasculated. The rot began, according to the renowned expert on trade law Professor John Jackson, because the United States was keen to support European integration on political grounds as a potential counterweight to the Soviet Union and its looming threat to Western Europe. When the European Common Market's imperfect union was formed and clearly was not in full conformity with Article 24 requirements, the United States looked the other way.[8] It also became progressively clear that bureaucrats could walk horses, if not elephants, through the ambiguities that clever lawyers could find and exploit in Article 24. What did it mean to say that "substantially all trade" must be covered—60 percent of trade, or 80 percent, or 90 percent? Would the reduction, at whatever percentage, have to be uniform and across the board, or could entire sectors, such as agriculture or high-tech, be left out? The "reasonable" length of time also turned

8. See Gerard Curzon, *Multilateral Commercial Diplomacy* (New York: Praeger, 1966), especially 266–68.

out to be a weak formulation. Later, in the 1994 Understanding on the Interpretation of Article 24 adopted at the GATT, the member states attempted to insert less weak language, to the effect that the period by which the PTA should be completed "should exceed 10 years only in exceptional cases," requiring merely that where this period was "insufficient," a full explanation was to be provided to the WTO Council on Trade in Goods.[9]

Indeed, over time, as the "disciplines" built into Article 24 frayed badly, there was a growing apprehension that Article 24 was likely to be an exception to MFN and its associated nondiscrimination in world trade that we may come to regret. Already by 1970, another great expert on trade law, Kenneth Dam, would write the following:

> The record is not comforting.... Perhaps only one of the more than dozen regional arrangements [i.e., PTAs] that have come before the GATT complied fully with Article XXIV criteria. That was the recent United Kingdom/Ireland Free Trade Area, and even in that case certain doubts were expressed before the working party [at the GATT to examine conformity of the proposed FTA to Article 24]. In some cases, the regional arrangements were very wide off the mark. The European Coal and Steel Community [the precursor to the European Common Market], covering only two major product lines, could not even qualify for the special regional-arrangement waiver of Article XXIV:10 but required a general waiver under Article XXV:5. The New Zealand/Australia Free Trade Agreement, although not purportedly an example of "functional integration," provided

9. A valuable analysis of the post-1994 "Legal Aspects of Free Trade Agreements in the Context of Article XXIV of the GATT" is provided by Professor Mitsuo Matsushita, the noted Japanese expert on trade law, in Mitsuo Matsushita and Ahn Dukgeun, eds., *WTO and East Asia: New Perspectives* (London: Cameron May, 2004).

for the liberalization of an even smaller percentage of intermember trade. A strong tendency has also been manifested for interim agreements to provide for an even longer transitional period and to contain increasingly fewer detailed commitments for eventual completion of the customs union or free-trade area.[10]

Indeed, as a result, even today, the question of whether the European Community (i.e., the European Union) fully (as distinct from "by and large") meets the Article 24 requirements is not without merit. Mindful of these departures from Article 24 discipline, the WTO has sought to strengthen scrutiny, and the exercise of genuine control, over new preferential trade agreements. Notably, in 1996, the WTO created the Committee on Regional Trade Agreements and charged it to examine whether the preferential trade agreements referred to it were compatible with Article 24. In recent years, the arrangements negotiated under Article 24 have improved somewhat, especially in the matter of substantial coverage. Increasing numbers of such PTAs seem to extend to all manufacturing items, and the time taken to trade freely among member countries has, broadly speaking, tended to converge in recent years to around 10 years, or occasionally a little more.[11] (Regional differences exist among the PTAs on the trajectories chosen for freeing trade. Some backload the reductions and others, especially in South America, frontload them.)[12]

10. Kenneth Dam, *The GATT: Law and International Economic Organization* (Chicago: University of Chicago Press, 1970), 290.

11. See Jo-Ann Crawford and Sam Laird, "Regional Trade Agreements and the WTO," Center for Research in Economic Development and International Trade, Research Paper, University of Nottingham, January 2000.

12. I am indebted to Kati Suominen, who has done extensive research on PTAs in the South American region, along with Antoni Estevadeordal and Matthew Shearer, for drawing my attention to this difference.

The fact remains, however, that, as the lawyer James Mathis has argued, the reviews at the WTO are more "political" than "judicial." They also constitute "executive action" with possible legal effect in later judicial reviews, although these have been rare.[13] In the end, the problem with Article 24, and the earlier GATT working parties and the later WTO Committee on Regional Trade Agreements (an inappropriate title, it may be recalled, since increasing numbers of PTAs, such as the U.S.-Israel FTA, cannot be described as "regional" in any meaningful manner) is that it is not easy to find political backing for stringent discipline when almost every member nation seems to be joining the fray. A stone cast at another is likely to be thrown back at oneself. Indeed, now that the PTAs have spread from Europe to the United States and then to Asia, there is virtually no country left that can play the leadership role in enforcing the discipline of Article 24, such as it is. The WTO watchdog has turned out to be a friendly poodle.

Third, the most disturbing disregard of Article 24 requirements has taken place for the developing countries. Increasingly during the 1970s, the developing countries sought and were accorded what came to be known as special and differential treatment (SDT). In essence, it meant that the developing countries were to be exempted in several ways from the obligations imposed by GATT membership, while enjoying the rights. This extended the asymmetric treatment within the GATT of the developing countries that had obtained already in trade negotiations in MTN rounds, where the

13. See Sydney Cone, "The Promotion of Free-Trade Areas Viewed in Terms of Most-Favored Nation Treatment and 'Imperial Preference,'" *Michigan Journal of International Law* 26 (2005): 569; and Mathis, *Regional Trade Agreements in the GATT/WTO*. With few exceptions, no member country has taken Article 24 cases to WTO panels.

developed countries were required to extend their tariff cuts to the developing countries but did not seek reciprocal tariff cuts.

The immediate cause of SDT was the Generalized System of Preferences (GSP), which provided one-way preferential access to eligible developing countries in the markets of the developed countries signing on to the scheme. Introduced in 1971 after an understanding reached at the United Nations Conference on Trade and Development (UNCTAD) in October 1970,[14] GSP was legally inconsistent with the MFN requirement. Earlier, in the 1960s, when a few developed countries had given SDT to selected developing countries, their inconsistency with the MFN requirement had been resolved in an ad hoc fashion by securing waivers (under Article 25). Such waivers being necessarily ad hoc, however, the developing countries requested and obtained, during the Tokyo Round negotiations, a Framework Group that was charged with the task of creating a permanent resolution to the SDT problem in regard to one-way preferences for the developing countries.

14. The UNCTAD, whose first secretary-general was Raul Prebisch, an eminent development economist from Argentina, was the original focal point for developmental concerns as they interacted with trade issues, and was thought of as a counterweight to the GATT in that regard. It did play a remarkable role in introducing a number of influential new ideas, including the first systematic analyses of tariff escalation, of trade in services, and of skilled migration flows, that have since entered multilateral trade negotiations and the working of the GATT itself. With the increased influence of the GATT, however, and the enhanced role of the developed countries within it, the role of the UNCTAD has been an issue. In 2006, the Group of Eminent Persons appointed by Director General Supachai under the chairmanship of former Brazilian president Hernando Cardoso, of which I was a member, reported on the future of the WTO. See the report, *Enhancing the Development Role and Impact of UNCTAD* (Geneva: UNCTAD, 2006) for an analysis of the issues that now face the UNCTAD.

That, in turn, led to what is known as the Enabling Clause, a decision by the contracting parties of the GATT.

The Enabling Clause legitimized the GSP scheme and other ways of granting one-way, nonreciprocal preferences to developing countries. It also provided legal cover for something altogether different: it opened the way for developing countries to escape the Article 24 obligations as well, as long as the PTA was "amongst less-developed contracting parties for the mutual reduction or elimination of tariffs . . . [and] non-tariff measures, on products imported from one another."[15]

Thus, as long as the member countries of a particular PTA do not include a developed country, the Enabling Clause permits developing countries to escape the discipline of Article 24 altogether. Specifically, the requirements that "substantially all trade" be covered or that there must be a definite commitment to elimination of all trade barriers are effectively eliminated; partial preferences, sectoral and less than 100 percent, can be exchanged at any level. It is an invitation to discrimination without discipline. Figure 2.1

15. Excellent statements on the history of SDT and the Enabling Clause can be found in several places. See, in particular, "The Future of Preferential Trade Arrangements for Developing Countries" (Geneva: Economic and Social Department, Food and Agriculture Organization of the United Nations, 2004); and Paul Kruger, "The Enabling Clause and the Article XXIV," *Tralac Newsletter*, June 13, 2006. But Mathis, *Regional Trade Agreements in the GATT/WTO*, 34–36, records that a precursor of the Enabling Clause is to be found in another weakening in the Havana Charter of the MFN requirement, other than that for FTAs, for preferences by "contiguous territories" or those belonging to the same "economic region" in the 1947 Geneva draft, Article 15, under the title "Preferential Agreements for Economic Development and Reconstruction." This article required neither reciprocity nor reduction of trade tariffs to zero, much like the Enabling Clause today. The article was not explicitly confined to developing countries, but its title suggests that it probably would have been if the ITO had been acceptable to the U.S. Senate.

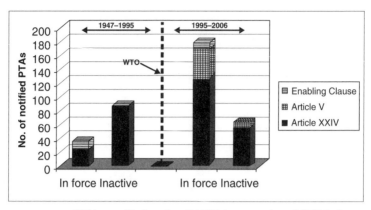

FIGURE 2.1. PTAs notified to the GATT (pre-1995) and WTO (post-1995)

Source: Trade Policy Review Division, World Trade Organization, Geneva, 2007.

shows the breakdown of GATT/WTO-notified PTAs into those invoking legitimacy under the 1979 Enabling Clause, Article 24 (GATT) and Article 5 (GATS). The estimated 30 unreported PTAs under the Enabling Clause are somewhat larger in number than the ones reported.[16]

The effective emasculation of Article 24 for developing nations has thus been a contributory factor in the proliferation of PTAs. That such a development is harmful to the developing countries that use the Enabling Clause is almost self-evident (and is discussed in chapter 3, on the consequences of the PTA proliferation today). But let me say immediately that the Enabling Clause has been justified by its proponents as reflecting the "need for policy space" for developing countries. My retort to this observation is this: Once a man shot himself in the foot and, when asked why he had done so, explained that he was exercising his "policy space."

16. Waivers also have been used, sparingly, to legitimate some PTAs.

THE IMPULSE TO FOLLOW EUROPEAN INTEGRATION: THE FIRST REGIONALISM

Even if the Enabling Clause had not been there, some developing countries would have exploited Article 24 in order to build their own regional PTAs among geographically proximate and historically bonded nations (as indeed they tried in East Africa and Latin America). What I have called the First Regionalism of the 1960s, as distinct from the Second Regionalism of the past two decades,[17] was precisely this. But it was hugely unsuccessful, in contrast to the Second Regionalism, which turned out to be excessively successful and resulted in the pandemic of PTAs today.

While the First Regionalism was certainly influenced by the European Community's first steps and the program of further steps toward full integration, its main impulse was altogether different. As industrialization became a major objective and the postwar policy of import substitution to promote industrialization took hold in most countries, it became obvious to the policy makers in the developing countries with small markets that attempts at producing everything in small quantities was extremely expensive. If they got together into a PTA and specialized among themselves, while maintaining tariff barriers against the rich countries in order to promote industrialization, that would reduce the cost of the import substitution policy. For example, if Tanzania, Kenya, and Uganda were *each* to produce small amounts of shoes, shirts, and bangles, the inability to exploit scale economies in production would send costs skyrocketing. If, instead, Tanzania made shoes, Kenya produced shirts, and Uganda specialized in bangles, and they then traded in these with each other, they would be able to

17. See Bhagwati, *The World Trading System at Risk,* chapter 5.

achieve the same amount of industrialization but at much lower cost because each would be able to exploit more scale economies.[18]

Despite a flurry of activity to launch an East African Common Market and the Latin American Free Trade Area, nothing transpired. Why? The reason was pretty simple. The developing countries in question wanted to allocate the different import-substituting activities among themselves by bureaucratic decisions and then support these allocations and intra-PTA specialization by managed trade, instead of liberalizing trade among themselves and letting the market decide who got what of the activities. The sheer difficulty of bureaucratic allocations, and the politics that would attend such decisions, got the whole effort mired in the mud. Trade should lead to production specialization; these PTAs tried to do it the other way around, putting the cart before the horse.

One may well ask: Why did the European Community example not lead other *developed* countries to attempt imitation? Here, the importance of decisive and principled U.S. leadership on nondiscrimination in trade, which has sadly collapsed in recent years (for reasons explored below), played a major role. Long suspicious of discriminatory trade arrangements, the United States restrained itself vigorously from using Article 24. The formation of the European

---

18. The theory behind this case for free trade agreements has been developed theoretically in the literature on PTAs. The early writers were C. A. Cooper and B. F. Massell, Harry Johnson, and myself. Later economists who provided a rigorous analysis were Arvind Panagariya and Pravin Krishna, who actually demonstrated ingeniously (using a theoretical insight of Murray Kemp and Henry Wan) that scale economies were not necessary in making a case for reducing the cost of a given value of import substitution in a subset of developing countries through a suitably designed customs union. References to their work, and a theoretically tight discussion of this approach, are provided in the graduate textbook by Bhagwati, Panagariya, and Srinivasan, *Lectures on International Trade*, in chapter 31. Also see the appendix.

Community in 1958 marked a partial watershed, but was meant to be little more than a chink in the U.S. armor. Entirely because the United States considered European cohesion and bonding to be a bulwark against the spreading Soviet stain, it did everything to see European integration through, negotiating around the several hoops that Article 24 imposed. Thus, the retention by the EU of discriminatory preferences for the 18 former colonies in Africa was allowed under a waiver that the United States supported. But if the United States backed the EU in this way, it was not in favor of the alternative European Free Trade Area, which was simply a discriminatory trade agreement, albeit under the auspices of Article 24.

The United States remained wedded to multilateralism and nondiscrimination in trade liberalization through the Kennedy Round. Regionalism, which makes sense because neighboring nations attract political attention, just as one's family will compel one's attention more than others more distant from oneself, was to be pursued through initiatives such as the Alliance for Progress (for South America). But these initiatives were in regard to nontrade matters such as support for democracy and provision of aid flows. On the other hand, trade was to be handled through the ongoing Kennedy Round, and the United States had no patience for PTAs, regardless of the ever-present temptation to exploit Article 24 for myopic gains.

THE SECOND REGIONALISM: NEW RATIONALES FOR PTAS

Although the spread of PTAs was facilitated by developments such as the emasculation of the Article 24 requirements and the enactment of the Enabling Clause, PTAs did not make headway because the U.S. political leadership was not willing to forget the lessons of the interwar period and sign on to trade discrimination. Where the First Regionalism floundered, the Second Regionalism since the early 1990s was a howling success (as is evident from Figures 1.2, 1.3, and 2.1). In fact, not only did the number of PTAs sharply accelerate, but several countries went beyond forming single PTAs and joined several, with a few countries jumping into several beds in a fit of preferential promiscuity. Thus, Mexico and the European Union wound up participating in more than ten PTAs each, and others, such as Brazil, Venezuela, and Chile, joined between five and ten. The resulting pattern of PTA participation (for goods) at the end of 2006 is seen in the world map in Figure 2.2.[19]

The complexity of the resulting trade regime is documented and its consequences are analyzed further in chapter 3. Let me now proceed to discuss the many elements that have contributed to this remarkable and deplorable turnaround that marks the Second Regionalism.

United States Changes Its Mind

Perhaps the principal cause of the Second Regionalism is the fact that the United States, which had abstained from pursuing its own bilaterals at the time of the First Regionalism, changed its mind and decided to abandon its policy of exclusive embrace of multilateralism in trade. It is worth remembering that, in the 1960s, there was already a small, but influential, movement to use Article 24 to launch a North Atlantic free trade agreement. But recall that this was the

19. This map is from the WTO Secretariat, as is Figure 2.1. Both are courtesy of Dr. Clemens Boonekamp, an accomplished economist who is the chief of the Trade Policies Review Division which reviews PTAs for the WTO. A similar map is available for PTAs for services from this Secretariat.

FIGURE 2.2. Participation in PTAs as of December 2006 (goods)

Source: Trade Policies Review Division, World Trade Organization Secretariat, Geneva, 2007.

▨ 1 to 4 ▦ 5 to 9 ▓ 10 to 19 ■ 20 to 26 ☐ No data

North *Atlantic* free trade area, not the current North American Free Trade Agreement among the United States, Canada, and Mexico, nor the New Zealand–Australian Free Trade Agreement—indeed, as scholars who know history, we must contend with an abundance of NAFTAs![20]

This first NAFTA had proponents who included prominent Atlanticists in the United States and in England.[21] Many of them were driven by a desire to create a countervailing liberal economic arrangement that would offset the European Community's leaning in a French socialist, anti–Anglo-Saxon direction. At the same time, many others in England, who were Europhiles, were pessimistic that the French would ever allow England to join the EC, and so England had no option, if it wanted a wider FTA or CU, but to go along with the United States and Canada. De Gaulle's opposition to British entry was very real and based on the fear that Britain would act as the Americans' Trojan horse, bringing into the EC fold the interests and influence of the United States and undermining the French policy of turning the EC into a bulwark against U.S. hegemony.

British Prime Minister Harold Wilson recalled in his *Memoirs* a 1965 cartoon from the English newspaper the *Observer* in which a diminutive Wilson says, "I even wake up tired!," to which a towering de Gaulle, a stethoscope in his ear, responds: "Hm. It's all those late night telephone calls to

---

20. The historical analysis that follows draws freely on my essay, "Beyond NAFTA: Clinton's Trading Choices," *Foreign Policy* 91 (Summer 1993): 155–62.

21. The proponents also included distinguished economists such as Harry Johnson, a Canadian, and prominent U.S. politicians such as Jacob Javits. Some even proposed that this NAFTA be extended later to include other, nontransatlantic nations, turning it into an FTA with the explicit ambition of reaching worldwide, multilateral free trade progressively and rapidly—a benign but unrealistic sentiment that has recurred time and again in the discussion of FTAs and their impact on the multilateral trading system.

Washington. What you need is an independent policy on Vietnam." Indeed, de Gaulle made no secret of his suspicions about the British. Thus, immediately before his resounding November 1967 rejection of British membership in the EC, de Gaulle queried Wilson on precisely that issue. As Wilson put it, "The whole situation would be very different if France were genuinely convinced that Britain really was disengaging from the U.S. in all major matters such as defense policy and in areas such as Asia, the Middle East, Africa and Europe."[22]

The reluctance of France to admit Britain into the European Union therefore imparted some momentum to the notion that the United States itself could provide a policy space for Britain and other English-speaking nations to do their own EU-style PTA formation around the United States. So the notion that the United States should totally abstain from using Article 24 was already being questioned by some.

EU Hub Seeking Spokes: United States Responds

The European Union played another role in undermining the U.S. abhorrence of Article 24. Few (and certainly not the United States) objected to the European "deep integration" model, in which intra-EU trade liberalization was seen as simply a part of the integration that the Europeans were undertaking to get as close as possible, more or less, to a United States of Europe. The "core" EU, expanding from six to 12 and now to 27 member states, could hardly be judged by narrow trade criteria: that would almost amount to the tail wagging the dog.

---

22. Harold Wilson, *Memoirs: The Making of a Prime Minister 1916–1964* (London: Weidenfeld and Nicolson and Michael Joseph, 1986).

Britain's entry into the European Common Market was desired by the United States to contain France, a fact that was understood by President de Gaulle, who regarded the British as a Trojan horse. In this cartoon, which appeared in *The Observer* (March 3, 1965), the Gaullist suspicions are illustrated in the context of Vietnam policy, with "Doctor" de Gaulle telling the tired patient, Prime Minister Harold Wilson, that his fatigue is due to the late-night calls to Washington.

But the hub represented by the EU core increasingly had a number of spokes, consisting of PTAs with non-EU members, all of which were primarily trade agreements. It had become fashionable for the EU commissioners to seek out such spokes, to mix metaphors, as feathers in their caps; in consequence, the spokes continued to expand. The EU practice can best be described as one of "the hub seeking spokes."

There is little doubt that, when the United States wound up abandoning its exclusive embrace of multilateralism in free trade, some of the trade negotiators had in mind the spectacle of the spokes voting on GATT issues with the hub. But this feeling was surely exaggerated: the voting pattern and the spokes were both to be explained instead by the neocolonial reach of countries like France into the heart of Africa, for instance. Besides, it was not unusual for the United States to be accused of having its own "foreign legion," especially in South America, with these regimes often ready to vote with the "imperial Yankees" even as many of their citizens condemned such dependence.

United States Offers Trade, Not Debt Relief, for South America

The U.S. move to PTAs, which began with the U.S.-Israel FTA (which is a purely political phenomenon that had nothing to do with economics, Israel being a special case in U.S. politics), was also prompted by yet another factor. Under Secretary of State James Baker, after NAFTA was launched, the United States decided to continue with PTAs in order to respond to growing pressures from South America for debt relief—then an anathema—by offering trade instead. "Trade, Not Aid," a popular slogan, was transformed, undoubtedly under pressure from the financial sector, into "Trade, Not Debt Relief." South America responded with willingness to get into PTAs, though only archival research will show whether this response was dictated by the United States or was an indigenous, independent reaction. In any event, the die was cast, and the United States became a hub for some spokes, which then were sought worldwide by Baker and his Deputy, Robert Zoellick (who would have a second inning as the U.S. trade representative under President George W. Bush, pushing for yet more PTAs in Morocco, Singapore, and Jordan). A PTA was offered to Egypt, for instance.

United States Seeks to Countervail Domestic Protectionism

Arguably another important driving force turned out to be a combination of two propositions. The first was that the U.S. situation in the 1980s under President Ronald Reagan was (sadly) protectionist because the dollar was seriously over-valued and protectionist bills were being introduced in droves. Reagan, no protectionist by temperament,[23] was being forced into throwing protectionist crumbs to the vociferous lobbies. But the crumbs were turning into loaves (as with the introduction of voluntary export restraints on Japan in 1981 for autos, limiting them to 2.2 million).[24]

It was imperative, according to Reagan's advisors, that until the exchange rate could be corrected (as happened with the 1985 Plaza Accord on exchange rates), the only way to countervail and contain the protectionists was to mobilize exporting interests by offering them markets abroad. But then the second proposition kicked in: the Europeans and the developing countries would not agree to declaring a new multilateral round when the United States tried hard to start one in 1982 (succeeding only in 1986, when the Uruguay Round was finally started with the Punta

23. President Reagan studied economics at Eureka College. But his senti-ment for free trade had little to do with his study of what economists such as myself wrote in favor of freer trade. It came, rather, from his belief in America's strength. Politicians rarely opt for free trade on cerebral grounds. Because freer trade leads to a Darwinian struggle for markets, those who believe that their businessmen will win will vote for freer trade. Here, the strong, un-nuanced belief in America's superiority on the part of both Presidents Reagan and George W. Bush has made them tilt strongly toward free trade, even as they had to make protectionist concessions from time to time.

24. President Reagan formally abandoned the VERs in 1985. But many economists believe that the Japanese continued to restrict exports nevertheless because they were persuaded that any increase in their auto exports would again trigger protectionist retaliation in the Congress.

del Este Ministerial Declaration in September 1986). The United States had concluded that it was left with no option except to go the bilateral route, which it did after protracted negotiation with the signing of the Canada-U.S. Free Trade Agreement in 1989.[25]

U.S. Directive of Walking on Two Legs

Once the overvaluation had been corrected and the Uruguay Round started, however, the United States persisted in its strategy of opening up the bilateral, preferential route. It made sense to go down the dirt road if the turnpike was closed. But we must ask why, once the turnpike was open, the United States persisted in making, and attempting to make, more PTA deals. Lack of leadership is one part of the answer. Robert Zoellick at the State Department and Fred Bergsten, the head of the Institute for International Economics, a Washington, D.C., think tank, both very able but neither a professional economist by training, wound up arguing that PTAs could be pursued simultaneously with multilateral trade negotiations, that one could walk on two legs (as the metaphor went), and that the PTAs would even serve to accelerate the MTNs and therefore act as what I have called "building blocks" rather than "stumbling blocks" to multilateral free trade. In truth, however, the attempt to walk on two legs resulted in walking on all fours: a chaotic, discriminatory world, which I describe and analyze in the next chapter. So, under the influence of defective reasoning, the United States joined in the rush to PTAs

---

25. Of course, the Uruguay Round negotiations were agreed to in 1986, three years before the actual agreement on the Canada United States Free Trade Agreement (CUFTA)! The PTAs game had begun, and neither the United States nor Canada was willing to abandon the game and concentrate on Geneva.

instead of exercising leadership and trying to throw sand into the EU bilaterals engine.

Bureaucratic and Ethnic Pressures in the United States

Bureaucratic reasons also helped. First, every bureaucrat who pursues these PTAs acquires high official rank, frequently that of ambassador. As PTAs multiply, so do the ranks of the bureaucrats acquiring titles. Second, bureaucrats who specialize, as they occasionally do in the State Department despite attempts at broadening their range, want PTAs for their own countries of interest. The South American expansion of U.S.-led PTAs has surely been blessed by the specialists within the U.S. administration who continually push for them, both when they are in the administration and when they are out and have joined think tanks in and outside of Washington. They continue to push for PTAs also when they become, as is often the case, lobbyists. (An acute example is the hiring at a high price by the Salinas administration in Mexico of Vice President Lloyd Bentsen's chief aide as the lead lobbyist for NAFTA.)[26] Third, once the pursuit of PTAs becomes an official policy, ethnic groups often join in the scramble, wanting PTAs for their own countries of origin. Thus, Indian businesspeople

26. The lobbying was so intense, and rumored to have cost the Salinas administration over US$25 million, that I remarked at the time: If Mexicans can play the U.S.-style lobbying game so effectively, it certainly qualifies them to join NAFTA! Indeed, the pro-NAFTA lobbying had also captured the media effectively, with a well-known economist actively pushing NAFTA boasting that he was close to President Salinas, who had given him an expensive painting which he displayed in his apartment. The media too had been flooded with propaganda in favor of NAFTA, to the point where at least one prominent news account of supporters of NAFTA included my name, when, in fact, I had refused to sign any petition for NAFTA.

in the United States have generally become proponents of a U.S.-India FTA.

Developing Countries Join In

Why have PTAs been multiplying in the developing countries as well? The reasons are diverse but can be differentiated by whether the developing countries are undertaking PTAs among themselves or with a hegemonic developed country or region such as the United States or the European Union.[27]

Intra-Developing-Country PTAs

Five factors motivate developing countries to form PTAs among themselves:

1. The reluctant liberalizers who feared competition from the developed countries felt that they should learn to compete with countries their own size, then go on to general free trade on an MFN basis. This might be called the "tricycle" theory: you need to learn how to ride a tricycle before you move on to a bicycle. There is no evidence, however, that developing countries have not managed, at suitable prices, to exploit trading opportunities. Just think back to South Korea at the time of the Korean War (a bunch of hamlets) and how Korea broke through into massive development via an extraordinary export performance that has taken it to membership in the Organization for Economic Co-operation and Development without the advantage of bilateral or preferential trade deals. Besides, in contrast to the tricycle theory,

---

27. The importance of distinguishing between intra-developing-country and hegemon-centered PTAs was first noted in Jagdish Bhagwati and Arvind Panagariya, "Preferential Trading Areas and Multilateralism—Strangers, Friends or Foes?," published originally in 1996 in a volume on PTAs by the American Enterprise Institute and edited by Panagariya and me. It has been reprinted as chapter 2 in Bhagwati, Krishna, and Panagariya, *Trading Blocs*.

you also have the analogy with swimming: being thrown into the water by your instructor is a bracing and effective way to learn how to swim. Or think of another analogy: your game will never improve if you play tennis only with those who are as bad as you. But analogies take you only so far; experience shows that competition does not require the third wheel on your bike. Nonetheless, it is a lesson that few are willing to accept, prompting some PTAs among nations that share low incomes.

2. Developing countries also share the view that bonding together into PTAs will improve their bargaining position in trade negotiations and, indeed, in international negotiations. There is little doubt that this was a motivating factor behind Mercosur, a customs union among Argentina, Brazil, Paraguay, and Uruguay, though it must be noted that, unlike the EU, where trade is negotiated at the level of the EU, Mercosur nations negotiate on their own.

3. Some of the middle-income developing countries have always been upset by the fact that multilateral trade negotiations, and their coverage by the media, have traditionally been focused on the EU trade commissioner and the U.S. trade representative, with even the big developing countries consigned to the sidelines. Forming their own PTAs give the smaller players a place in the sun, even if on their home ground. From this perspective, it is important that the coalition of bigger developing countries, G-20, materialized in the Cancun WTO meeting over the Doha Round negotiations, even if Mr. Zoellick seemed irritated by this development: it gave these countries a political stake in the multilateral trade negotiations.

4. There is the "monkey see, monkey do" factor. If many others are doing PTAs, you do them too; so many cannot be doing something wrong. It also becomes particularly hard, when the EU and the United States are proliferating PTAs, to go to your trade minister and your prime minister and tell them that they should not create some PTAs of their own: they are likely to ask you to return to the university you teach at!

5. Ignoring the fact that it is the PTAs that are helping to undermine the multilateral trade negotiations by diverting political and bureaucratic energies and pro-trade lobbies away from multilateral trade negotiations (as I argue in the next chapter), many developing countries increasingly cite "insurance" against the possible failure of the multilateral Doha Round as the reason to pursue PTAs. This argument was best articulated by Singapore's prime minister Lee Hsien Loong when he spoke at the Asian-Pacific Economic Cooperation Conference in Vietnam in November 2006. Saying "We cannot eat disk drives" and that FTAs are necessary to "assure us of our trading links," he explained, "[With the Doha Round in limbo,] we need to buy insurance and the way we buy insurance is to negotiate bilateral free trade agreements with our major trading partners.... In case the world trading system runs into trouble, I have my access to these markets assured by a bilateral agreement."[28]China has expressed similar sentiments as it multiplies PTAs of its own. But whereas Singapore's argument seems specious—if Doha does not settle in the next few years, there is no reason to think that protectionism will break out, so it is unclear what the insurance is for—the Chinese concern is more realistic since, despite its WTO entry, it is still vulnerable to substantial market-denying possibilities via antidumping and other harassments. Insurance through special bilateral deals gives China an element of assurance that it probably needs and values.

Hegemon-Centered PTAs

When developing countries form PTAs with a hegemonic power, the motivations can be different from the motivations behind forming PTAs among themselves. They need further to be distinguished into those that motivate the

28. See, for instance, the report posted on November 24, 2006, on bilaterals.org, which is a collective effort to share information and to stimulate cooperation against bilateral agreements.

developing countries and those that characterize the hegemon itself. Consider the following six arguments.

1. For some developing countries, the main motivation to form a
   PTA is security. Thus, Singapore's leadership does not hide the
   fact that its FTA with the United States is dictated largely by a
   desire to keep the United States involved in the region. I might
   paraphrase colorfully the substance of what former prime minister
   Lee Kuan Yew told me many years ago: Japan was wicked in Asia
   during World War II; China will be wicked when the time is
   ripe; and we cannot afford to have the United States withdraw
   from Asia. Similarly, the U.S.–South Korea FTA has been
   prompted by security reasons: with China to its west, Japan to its
   east, and North Korea to its north, South Korea has a keen interest in keeping the United States as its trading partner and ally,
   even as the young South Koreans often express anti-American
   sentiments.

2. The proponents of hegemon-centered PTAs have also argued
   that such a PTA provides them with credibility that their economic reforms will stay in place, thus attracting kudos and capital.
   Therefore, during NAFTA negotiations Mexico expressed the
   view that the credibility of its overall economic reforms would be
   assured, and that these reforms would further be "locked in" by
   the treaty since it would be hard to unravel NAFTA, with its
   attendant trade liberalization within the region, once it was in
   place. The first argument seems to be exaggerated because
   Mexico simultaneously signed on to the GATT, which also can
   be a source of credibility in Mexico's reforms. Besides, a whole
   host of factors, such as whether the leadership seems able to
   implement the announced reforms and stay the course, will determine the credibility of reforms, not just whether NAFTA or
   GATT is in place! The second argument has some merit: NAFTA
   would indeed be hard to reverse once it is in place (though sabre-
   rattling against NAFTA by Senators Clinton and Obama in their

bid for the Democratic nomination in 2008 somewhat under-
mines that claim). But it does prompt an interesting question: Is it
really democratic to have President Salinas (who signed NAFTA)
tie the hands of future Mexican presidents in this way? We know
that Ulysses was wise to tie his hands before sailing past the sirens,
but here we have Ulysses tying the hands of others.

3. As Richard Baldwin in particular has emphasized, some developing countries want to join an FTA with a hegemon who is
signing such FTAs with others, simply because they fear that
otherwise they will suffer from trade diversion in the hegemon's
market to these other suppliers. Malaysia and Singapore, among
others, have expressed this motivation. Whether this rationale
works depends, however, on the ability of the existing FTA
partners to prevent the erosion of their privileged, preferential
access through the admission of others to an FTA with the hegemon and whether that will create a sufficiently countervailing
force to deny such trade-diversion erosion.

4. Contrasting with the "trade-diversion-eliminating" motivation
for creating a PTA, there is also "tit-for-tat" motivation for
creating a PTA that "retaliates" against another PTA. This is a
plausible, partial explanation of why the United States expanded
its own PTAs when the European Union began expanding its
"spokes." More recently, we have another example that is equally
compelling. When the United States decided to open up FTAs
such as NAFTA and then decided to go south with a view to
creating a Free Trade Agreement of the Americas, Asians were
not invited to participate in these PTAs. As a result, the current
plans of the Association of Southeast Asian Nations (ASEAN) for
PTAs, such as ASEAN+1, ASEAN+3, and ASEAN+6, do not
include the United States and have been Asia-centered. The
United States therefore is concerned that when it opted for South
America, an economically sluggish and volatile region, it lost the
far more dynamic Asian region. The result has been a frantic effort
on the part of the Office of the U.S. Trade Representative, acting

President Alan García of Peru announcing the agreement, with Congressman Rangel and Senator Levine virtually dictating the legislative language to Peru, over the incorporation of approved labor standards in Peruvian law, imposed by the U.S. Congress as a precondition for approval of the Peru-U.S. FTA. *Embassy of Peru in Washington, D.C.*

also through friends such as Fred Bergsten, to push for a Free Trade Area of the Asia-Pacific, under APEC auspices, urging that Asia and the Pacific (i.e., the United States, of course) nations of APEC not be divided!

6. Hegemons' biggest motivation to favor the PTA over the multilateral route for freeing trade has been the use of their PTAs to advance trade-unrelated agendas. Lobbies in the United States, in particular, have successfully pressured the U.S. administration and Congress into negotiations with weaker powers one-on-one for a variety of concessions in trade-unrelated areas of central concern to them. Such concessions have been a precondition for FTA approval. The latest example is the way Peru was forced into making changes in its labor laws prior to getting its FTA with the

United States approved by Democrats in Congress. Recent photographs documenting that congressional coup were quite revealing: Peruvian president Alan García, a once proud student of the French left-wing philosopher and activist Regis Debray and a socialist, virtually kowtows to Representative Charles Rangel and Senator Carl Levine of the "capitalist" and "neo-imperialist" United States as they approve Peru's FTA. The congressmen grin like viceroys of a metropolitan power dictating to their colonies.

Led by the AFL-CIO, the labor lobbies and other lobbies wanting restrictions on the use of capital controls during financial crises and restrictions on intellectual property protection going well beyond the agreement at the WTO, to take only two examples, have now captured U.S. trade policy. How they have done so, and the consequences of this for the world trading system and for the developing countries, are the subjects of the analysis in the next chapter.

CHAPTER 3

Why PTAs Are a Pox on the World Trading System

The worries over PTAs have increased dramatically in the past two decades as PTAs have proliferated. What exactly are the downsides of this phenomenon, which has gathered speed and become an addiction of the politicians, even as economists (with few exceptions) have expressed alarm at the development? What exactly are they worried about?

TRADE DIVERSION

The traditional objection to PTAs was simply that, as stated in the previous chapter, they could divert trade from the cost-efficient nonmember countries to the relatively inefficient member countries. The reason, of course, is that the nonmembers continue to pay the pre-PTA tariffs, whereas the higher cost member countries no longer have to.

It is easy to see that such a shift in production to a higher cost member country must sabotage the efficient allocation among countries and thus undermine what economists call "world welfare," or, in more palatable language, "cosmo-politan advantage." Recall that Jacob Viner was the first to draw attention to the possibility of trade diversion arising with discriminatory reduction of trade barriers in PTAs. He had focused mainly on PTAs' impact on cosmopolitan ad-vantage, but it was pretty obvious to economists that such trade discrimination could hurt the liberalizing country it-self. Why? Because when a country (call it the "home" country) shifts to a higher cost within-the-PTA supplier, it is buying its imports more expensively, incurring what econ-omists call a "terms of trade" loss.

Trade diversion is not a slam-dunk argument against PTAs, for offsetting the loss from trade diversion can be a gain if trade creation takes place. Trade may grow because consumers in the home country now pay lower prices in their own markets; the higher cost supply from the member country is still cheaper than what the domestic consumers had to pay before the PTA was formed. Again, the import-competing producers in the home country will reduce their own inefficient production as the domestic price of imports falls after the PTA comes into operation; this also leads to welfare-enhancing trade creation. Therefore, whether a specific trade-diverting PTA brings loss or gain to a country depends on the relative strengths of the trade diversion and trade creation effects.[1]

The really important implication of the "trade diversion" analysis, however, was that informed economists could no longer pretend that it did not matter how one liberalized trade, that preferential trade liberalization was possibly a

---

1. This analysis of trade diversion and creation is in a simplified framework, designed to convey the essence of the trade-diversion issues raised by PTAs. For a theoretically tight treatment, the reader is referred to the extended analysis by Panagariya and me in Bhagwati, Krishna, and Panagariya, *Trading Blocs,* chapter 2.

Jacob Viner (1892–1970), a Canadian economist who taught at Chicago and at Princeton, was one of the great economists of his time, and arguably the leading international trade economist of his generation. He pioneered the analysis of PTAs by noting that they could lead to trade diversion and be harmful to both the members of the PTA and to worldwide efficiency of resource allocation. *Princeton University Archives, Department of Rare Books and Special Collections, Princeton University Library.*

two-edged sword on which one could impale oneself. Thus, when some policy makers said that all trade liberalization was good, whether it was through bilateralism, plurilateralism, or multilateralism, they were really flying in the face of science and lacked credibility as much as someone who asserted that, if you wanted to raise revenue, it did not matter what kind of taxes you imposed. Indeed, as I told Larry Summers, the brilliant economist who was indulgent toward PTAs when he was vice president of the World Bank before he became the U.S. Treasury secretary and expressed impatience with concerns over trade diversion: "If I was asked to advise the Treasury in Washington, D.C., and argued that all taxes were equally acceptable, would you not summarily ask me to return to Columbia, where I could do less damage?"

As it happens, the proponents of PTAs are too complacent about the phenomenon of trade diversion. Consider seven principal arguments.

1. There is evidence of fierce competition in many products and sectors today, with few managing to escape with "thick" margins of competitive advantage that provide comforting buffers against loss of comparative advantage.[2] Thus, even small tariffs are compatible with trade diversion as tariffs are removed from members of a PTA while they remain in place on nonmembers.

2. The thinness of comparative advantage also implies that today we have what I have called kaleidoscopic comparative advantage, or what in jargon we economists call "knife-edge" comparative advantage. Countries can easily lose comparative advantage to some "close" rivals, who may be from any number of foreign suppliers. So even if preferences today do not lead to trade diversion, the menu of products where you develop comparative

---

2. I have discussed the reasons for this phenomenon and its consequence for coping with globalization in my book, *In Defense of Globalization* (New York: Oxford University Press, 2007), afterword.

advantage in a world of volatility and rapidly shifting comparative advantage will be forever changing, and any given preferences may lead to trade diversion in the near future, if not today.

3. While Article 24 requires that the external tariffs not be raised when the PTA is formed so as not to harm nonmembers,[3] the fact is that they can be raised when the external (MFN) tariffs are bound at higher levels than the actual tariffs. In these cases, a member of the PTA is free to raise the external MFN tariffs up to the bound levels, whereas typically the scheduled tariff reductions in the PTA, when a hegemonic power is involved, will be hard to suspend.[4] This is in fact what happened during the Mexican peso crisis of 1994, when external tariffs were raised on 502 items from 20 percent or less to as much as 35 percent, while the NAFTA-defined reductions in Mexican tariffs on U.S. and Canadian goods continued. So the prospect of trade diversion actually increased, despite the intent of those who drafted Article 24.

4. Article 24 freezes only external tariffs when the PTA is formed, with no increase in the external tariff allowed. But it does not

3. This restriction is compatible with trade diversion even when the external terms of trade are inflexible and the damage is to the member rather than the nonmember countries. But the nonmember countries also can be hurt when the terms of trade are variable. The empirical evidence of such nonmember terms-of-trade effects is provided in W. Chang and Alan Winters, "How Regional Blocs Affect Excluded Countries: The Price Effects of MERCOSUR," *American Economic Review* 92, no. 4 (2001). Recent theoretical work by Masahiro Endoh, Koichi Hamada, and Koji Shimomura, "Can a Preferential Trade Agreement Benefit Neighbor Countries without Compensating Them?" unpublished manuscript, Yale University, December 2007, demonstrates in fact that PTAs, unless accompanied by tariff concessions or compensatory transfers, will generally speaking hurt nonmember countries under reasonable restrictions.

4. As Petros Mavroidis has reminded me, when PTAs are formed under Article 24, the members of the PTA are free to raise their external tariffs from the applied levels to the higher bound levels. So the discipline on external tariffs essentially does not operate when the bound levels are higher than the applied tariffs, which is almost always the case, though in varying degrees for different countries.

address the modern reality that "administered protection" (i.e., antidumping and other actions by the executive) is both elastic and can be used and abused more or less freely in practice. Once you take into account the fact that trade barriers can take the form of antidumping measures, which are arbitrary in their design and protectionist in their practice, there is a real danger that initially welfare-enhancing trade creation can be transformed into harmful trade diversion through antidumping actions taken against nonmembers. Thus, if a member country is gaining a market in the member "home" country, creating trade by replacing inefficient home country production with less inefficient production and imports from another member country, that pressure could be accommodated, not by allowing domestic industry to yield to these imports from a member country, but by discouraging imports from the nonmember countries by using antidumping actions against them. Thus trade-creating imports from member countries could be replaced by trade-diverting restrictions on imports from nonmember countries.

Such an "endogenous" response of the external trade barriers, typically in the shape of antidumping actions, violates the spirit of Article 24, which explicitly prohibits trade barriers on nonmembers from being raised but is confined to tariffs and does not extend to "administered protection."[5]

5. There is plenty of evidence that trade diversion can occur through content requirements placed on member countries to establish "origin" so as to qualify for the preferential duties. Thus, typically, to qualify for the preferential tariffs in PTAs that include the United States, one must satisfy requirements such as that the imports of raw materials and components must come from the

---

5. This was initially noted by me in "Regionalism and Multilateralism: An Overview," in De Melo and Panagariya, *New Dimensions in Regional Integration.* It has been developed fully in Bhagwati and Panagariya, "Preferential Trading Areas and Multilateralism:—Strangers, Friends or Foes?," 64–66.

United States. For example, if apparel exports to the United States are accorded preferential tariffs, they must be made with U.S. textiles. This naturally diverts trade in textiles from efficient nonmember suppliers to inefficient U.S. textile producers.

6. Many analysts do not understand the distinction between trade diversion and trade creation and simply take all trade increase as welfare-enhancing. However, some recent analysts who are familiar with the phenomenon of trade diversion have tried to estimate it using what is called the "gravity model." Dating back some decades, this equation simply explains trade between two countries as a function of income and distance. Adapting this simple equation to their use, the economists Jeffrey Frankel and Shang-Jin Wei, who pioneered the use of gravity analysis to estimate trade creation and trade diversion, estimated total bilateral trade between any pair of countries as a function of their income and per capita incomes, with bilateral distance accounted for by statistical procedures.[6] If the countries belonged to, say, the Western hemisphere and they traded more with each other than with a random pair of countries located outside the region, that would mean that the PTA between countries in the Western hemisphere had led to trade creation. But it is clear that even if one disregards other objections, the real problem with the analysis is that more trade between partners in a PTA can take place with *both* trade creation and trade diversion, so that one simply cannot infer trade creation alone from this procedure. Hence, the recent estimates based on gravity equation, which are improved variations on the original Frankel-Wei approach and which sometimes (but not always) suggest that PTAs in practice have led to more trade creation than diversion, cannot be treated

---

6. In technical terms, the Frankel-Wei estimating equation uses dummy variables that take a value of 1 if both countries are in Western Europe and zero otherwise. I am grateful to Arvind Panagariya, who took me through the statistical procedures and their rather drastic limitations, in both the original Frankel-Wei analysis and its later variants by themselves, Gary Hufbauer, and others.

as reliable guides to the problem of determining whether or not a PTA has led to trade diversion.[7]

7. Several economists have suggested that we need not worry about trade diversion and that beneficial effects will prevail if PTAs are undertaken with "natural trading partners." The initial proponents of this idea, Paul Wonnacott and Mark Lutz, declared, "Trade creation is likely to be great and trade diversion small if the prospective members of an FTA are natural trading partners."[8] One criterion proposed for saying that PTA partners are natural trading partners is the volume of trade already between them; the other is geographic proximity. Neither really works.[9]

At the outset, note that though some writers, including Paul Krugman and Larry Summers, both heavy hitters, have occasionally argued as if the two criteria go together, they do not. There is no evidence that pairs of contiguous countries or countries with common borders have larger volumes of trade with each other than do pairs that are not so situated, or that trade volumes of pairs of countries arranged by distance between the countries in the pair will also show distance to be inversely related to trade volumes.[10] This is evident from Table 3.1, which contains

7. Some economists have posed the question of the welfare effects directly by using computable general equilibrium (CGE) models to compare the welfare outcomes under different trade policies, such as multilateral free trade under the Doha Round and current and potential preferential trade agreements. Using the Michigan CGE model of world production and trade developed by Robert Stern, Alan Deardorff, and Drusilla Brown, the economists Kozo Kiyota and Stern have calculated that the gains under multilateral trade liberalization dominate significantly those from a policy of PTAs.

8. Paul Wonnacott and Mark Lutz, "Is There a Case for Free Trade Areas?," in Jeffrey Schott, ed., *Free Trade Areas and U.S. Trade Policy* (Washington D.C.: Institute for International Economics, 1989).

9. The following discussion draws on the far more thorough analysis of the "natural trading partner" hypothesis by Panagariya and me in Bhagwati, Krishna, and Panagariya, *Trading Blocs,* chapter 2.

10. This would generally be true, I am sure, even if one were to take the measure just for one individual country with every other country instead of

destination-related trade volume for major regions in 1980, 1985, and 1990.[11] There are some compelling examples. Chile shares a common border with Argentina, but in 1993 it shipped only 6.2 percent of exports to and received only 5 percent of imports from Argentina.[12] By contrast, the United States does not share a common border with Chile, nor are the two countries close geographically. Yet in 1993, the United States accounted for 16.2 percent of Chilean exports and 24.9 percent of its imports. The volume-of-trade criterion would thus make the United States, not Argentina, Chile's natural trading partner, clearly contradicting the claim that the volume-of-trade criterion translates into the regional criterion, even in a broad-brush sense. The two criteria, and their inappropriateness in ensuring that trade diversion will be mini-mized and beneficial effects of the PTA guaranteed, must therefore be assessed separately, as immediately below.

Natural Trading Partners: Volume of Trade Criterion

First, there is a problem of intransitivity when we use this criterion. Country A may have a large share of its trade with Country B, but for Country B, Country A may be of negligible importance in trade. Country A and Country B are therefore natural trading partners or not, depending on which country's trade shares are taken into consideration.

---

pooling all possible pairs together. I might add that the gravity equation that shows distance to matter for the volume of trade is taking only a "partial de-rivative," so to speak, with regard to distance; the discussion in the text relates instead, as is proper in the matter of the equation of the "volume of trade" and "geographical proximity" by Krugman and Summers, simply to the relationship between distance and observed trade volumes.

11. For the table and for further discussion of the issues, see Bhagwati and Panagariya, "Preferential Trading Areas and Multilateralism—Strangers, Friends or Foes?" 59–61.

12. See Arvind Panagariya, "The Free Trade Area of the Americas: Good for Latin America?" *World Economy* 19, no. 5 (1996), Tables 3 and 4.

TABLE 3.1 Direction of Exports by Major Regions, 1980, 1985, and 1990

Exporter	Year	Partner							
		North America	Western Europe	Europe	East Asia[a]	Latin America	Africa	Middle East	South Asia
North	1980	33.5	25.2	27.4	15.8	8.9	3.3	4.2	1.0
America	1985	44.4	19.3	21.0	15.5	5.9	2.5	3.2	1.0
	1990	41.9	22.3	23.4	20.4	5.0	1.7	2.6	0.8
Western	1980	6.7	67.1	71.9	2.9	2.4	7.2	5.5	0.7
Europe	1985	11.3	64.9	68.9	3.6	1.6	5.2	5.0	0.9
	1990	8.3	71.0	74.4	5.3	1.1	3.3	3.3	0.7
Europe	1980	6.3	63.7	72.7	2.7	2.3	6.9	5.5	0.7
	1985	11.0	63.5	69.2	3.4	1.6	5.1	5.0	0.9
	1990	8.2	70.6	74.5	5.2	1.1	3.3	3.3	0.7
East Asia	1980	26.0	16.8	18.9	29.9	4.1	4.4	7.4	1.8
	1985	37.8	13.6	15.5	25.3	2.8	2.2	5.1	2.0
	1990	31.9	19.8	20.7	32.3	1.9	1.6	3.0	1.5
Latin	1980	27.9	26.5	35.1	5.4	16.6	2.7	1.9	0.5
America	1985	35.8	25.9	30.4	7.1	12.1	3.7	3.0	0.7
	1990	22.9	25.3	27.6	10.3	14.0	2.1	2.4	0.4
Africa	1980	27.4	43.6	46.1	4.3	3.2	1.8	1.7	0.3
	1985	14.8	64.9	69.3	1.8	4.2	5.1	2.2	0.7
	1990	3.0	66.0	68.0	4.6	0.6	12.8	4.4	3.6
Middle	1980	11.5	40.3	41.5	28.7	5.0	1.5	4.1	2.5
East	1985	6.2	15.0	17.7	1.5	0.3	1.4	8.7	0.4
	1990	17.8	48.6	53.0	9.1	1.2	3.6	8.5	0.9
South	1980	10.9	24.6	39.4	14.5	0.5	6.8	14.5	5.6
Asia	1985	18.4	20.8	37.0	16.4	0.4	4.6	11.0	4.4
	1990	17.1	30.1	46.6	18.3	0.3	2.7	6.5	3.2

a. East Asia does not include China.

Source: Jagdish Bhagwati, Pravin Krishna, and Arvind Panagariya, eds., *Trading Blocs: Alternative Approaches to Analyzing Preferential Trade Agreements* (Cambridge, Mass.: MIT Press, 1999).

This is reminiscent of the gag where a man pleased with himself and the precision of his language says, "I am his best friend, but he is not mine."

Second, the notion that higher volume of trade reflects "natural" outcomes is not persuasive. In truth, the high volume need not be "natural" in any meaningful sense. Thus, arrangements such as offshore assembly processing (OAP) have biased imports into the United States toward Mexico because, under OAP, the duty charged by the United States on processed goods in the maquiladoras in Mexico alongside the Rio Grande is reduced pro rata to content that is imported from the United States. Again, the U.S.-Canada bilateral free trade zone for cars, sanctioned by the GATT, was a "carve-out" that was not extended on an MFN basis to other car producers worldwide; it clearly added "unnaturally" to U.S.-Canada trade. Also, the grant of one-way preferences under the GSP schemes by the rich countries has been biased, through choice of products among other ways, toward specific regions of political interest to the rich countries extending the GSP benefits, thus biasing trade volumes artificially again. Those who believe that an initial high trade volume implies that the additional trade prompted by a PTA will be free from trade diversion are then inferring potential trade creation from previous trade diversion.

Third, however, it is generally a mistake to predict what will happen at the margin from what characterizes the average, that is, the initial situation. There is really no presumption to that effect. It is easy to construct models showing, for example, that preferential tariff reductions are beneficial up to a certain range and then begin, as barriers are further reduced, to create losses at the margin. So inferring a gain at the margin just because there was a gain earlier can be quite wrong. Or consider the fact that a shift in comparative advantage—a likely situation in today's world of volatile, kaleidoscopic comparative advantage, as I argued earlier—could mean a shift across industries; then trade creation turns, in one or more sectors, into trade diversion, despite the volume of trade being high and unchanged. The fact that comparative advantage is not frozen at a static level means that any assurance derived from the initial high volume of trade among countries undertaking a PTA is no guarantee against trade diversion resulting from shifting comparative advantage.

Natural Trading Partners: Distance or "Transport Cost" Criterion

If the volume-of-trade criterion is inappropriate as sufficient to make PTAs beneficial, can we choose PTA members by using transport cost or (economic) distance as a way to eliminate trade diversion? This is not a valid proposition either. It is enough to produce a counterexample to destroy this assertion. This has been done by Panagariya and myself: we showed that a PTA between Country A and a more distant partner, Country B, produces more gain for A than does a PTA between Country A and less distant Country C.[13]

Although trade diversion is therefore not to be considered a "theoretical curiosum," and is certainly not a piece of scholarly exotica that can be ignored or readily avoided, economists have suggested ways that trade diversion may be minimized by modifications to Article 24, an issue I discuss in chapter 4.

---

13. The counterexample has been fully set out in Bhagwati and Panagariya, "Preferential Trade Areas—Strangers, Friends or Foes?," 62–64.

THE "SPAGHETTI BOWL": A SYSTEMIC CONCERN

The Vinerian concerns about the trade diversion that a PTA can cause have yielded by now to "systemic" concerns about PTAs; their proliferation has meant that we cannot pretend any longer that we are analyzing only isolated PTAs as, without doubt, the original architects of Article 24 in the GATT must have thought about the matter.

The systemic problem from discriminatory trade liberalization under PTAs arises in two ways. First, when a country enters into multiple FTAs, it is evident that the same commodity will be subjected to different tariff rates if, as is almost always the case, the trajectories of tariff reduction vary for different FTAs.[14] Second, and much more important, is the overriding fact that, with PTAs, tariffs on specific commodities must depend on where a product is supposed to originate (requiring inherently arbitrary "rules of origin").

With PTAs proliferating, the trading system can then be expected to become chaotic. Crisscrossing PTAs, where a nation had multiple PTAs with other nations, each of which then had its own PTAs with yet other nations, was inevitable. Indeed, if one only mapped the phenomenon, it would remind one of a child scrawling a number of chaotic lines on a sketch pad. An early sketch of the "spaghetti bowl" for Europe is reproduced in Figure 3.1.

---

14. At the end, when the PTA has reached free trade, the tariffs are eliminated in principle. So when all PTAs by a country have terminated, the problem of different tariffs on the same commodity, depending on which PTA it is imported from, would disappear. But against this comforting scenario, consider that in practice enduring exceptions are made in important sectors, including sectoral exemptions and via use of tariff quotas and quantitative restrictions where WTO-compatible. Also, all PTAs are not signed on the same day, so tariff differences on different origins can persist for long periods indeed.

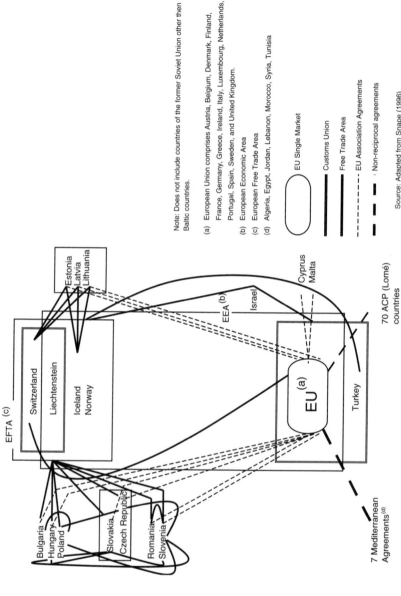

Note: Does not include countries of the former Soviet Union other then Baltic countries.

(a) European Union comprises Austria, Belgium, Denmark, Finland, France, Germany, Greece, Ireland, Italy, Luxembourg, Netherlands, Portugal, Spain, Sweden, and United Kingdom.
(b) European Economic Area
(c) European Free Trade Area
(d) Algeria, Egypt, Jordan, Lebanon, Morocco, Syria, Tunisia

⬭ EU Single Market

—— Customs Union

—— Free Trade Area

------ EU Association Agreements

– – – Non-reciprocal agreements

Source: Adapted from Snape (1996)

EFTA (c)
Switzerland
Liechtenstein
Iceland
Norway

Estonia
Latvia
Lithuania

Bulgaria
Hungary
Poland
Slovakia
Czech Republic
Romania
Slovenia

EEA (b)

Israel

Cyprus
Malta

EU (a)

Turkey

70 ACP (Lomé) countries

7 Mediterranean Agreements (d)

FIGURE 3.1. The European spaghetti bowl and key.

Source: Jagdish Bhagwati, David Greenaway, and Arvind Panagariya, "Trading Preferentially: Theory and Policy," *Economic Journal*, July 1998, figure 3.

Soon it had become an industry: see a recent illustration of Asia in Figure 3.2 that is equally disturbing. The global map of PTAs by region, produced by the British economist Christopher Dent, a foremost analyst of PTAs today, is provided in Figure 3.3.

Crisscrossing PTAs, causing in turn the mish-mash of preferential trade barriers, prompted me to christen them the "spaghetti bowl" phenomenon and problem, I guess because I cannot eat spaghetti without dropping it on my tie and shirt. I once used the phrase in an after-dinner speech; my Italian host, who had no trouble eating spaghetti, was nonplussed.

The phrase has caught on famously.[15] Thus, Australia's impressive ambassador to the WTO, Geoffrey Raby, alarmed by the accelerating growth of PTAs, once told me, "Jagdish, your spaghetti bowl is getting worse; instead of pesto sauce, we now have diesel oil and nails with the spaghetti." Then again, in the Far East, and in the context of Asian PTAs, it is now referred to as the "noodle bowl," and each PTA that contributes to the chaos is called a "noodle."[16] Of course, Marco Polo is reputed to have brought noodles, eaten since the Han Dynasty, back from China, giving us the Italian spaghetti. So perhaps this Asian shift of terminology from spaghetti to noodles is only a matter of extended reciprocity spanning two millennia.

15. When I gave a talk at the WTO in July 2007, presided over by Pascal Lamy, the director general of the WTO, he said that he had downloaded references to spaghetti and found that I was right there with my spaghetti bowl alongside different types of spaghetti (as noted in the next chapter), making me the only well-known economist also to have culinary recognition! I responded by saying that, from a Frenchman who must pride himself on the extraordinary success of his country's cuisine, that must be considered a real compliment.

16. The phrase was introduced by President Haruhiko Kuroda of the Asian Development Bank in July 2006 in a speech delivered to the Jeju Summer Forum in South Korea.

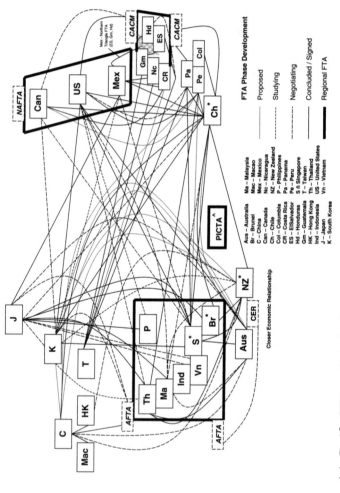

FIGURE 3.2. Asia–Pacific FTA projects (by June 2007).

Notes: ★ Pacific-3 FTA expands to quadrilateral Trans-Pacific Strategic Economic Partnership (TPSEPA) project, including Brunei as full negotiating partner from April 2005. PICTA (Pacific Island Countries Trade Agreement) involves the 14 Pacific Island Countries.

Source: Drawn and supplied by Christopher Dent.

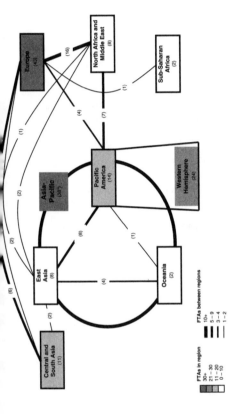

FIGURE 3.3. Global map of FTAs by region (by end of 2005).

Notes: 1. Figures relate to FTAs signed under WTO Article 24 and do not include partial scope agreements under the WTO's Enabling Clause for developing countries or Service Agreements under WTO Article 5.

2. Pacific America comprises those Western Hemisphere countries with a Pacific Ocean coastline. Central and South Asia include the Russia and Asian former Soviet republics, as well as the Commonwealth of Independent States FTA. Europe includes the former Soviet republics of Belarus, Moldova, and Ukraine.

3. Figures include customs unions. By this time, Europe was host to four customs union agreements (European Union, EU–Malta, EU–Cyprus, and EU–Andorra), and the EU also had a customs union with Turkey. Similarly, the Western Hemisphere region was host to four customs unions (CAN, CACM, Caricom, and Mercosur), Central Asia to one (EAEC), and sub-Saharan Africa to one (SACU).

★ Trans–Pacific Strategic Economic Partnership (TPSEPA) FTA between Singapore, Chile, New Zealand, and Brunei counted as an additional FTA link.

Source: Drawn and supplied by Christopher Dent.

The chaos resulting from arbitrary rules of origin, designed to establish which product is whose—what I have called the "who is whose" question (reminding me of my undergraduate days at Cambridge, where some mischievously gossipy students used to bring out a "who is whose" guide to amorous relationships on campus)—would be considerable even if the rules of origin were unique and uniformly applied. Typical rules of origin require what are called "substantial transformation" tests to decide whether a product is eligible for the preferential tariff rate. Thus, if a Canadian product is to be certified as eligible for NAFTA preferential tariffs when entering the U.S. market, and it uses imported components or raw materials (e.g., Honda in Canada uses steel that may be imported), the product must generally satisfy one of the following criteria:

1. A change in tariff classification: Under the Harmonized System of Tariffs (which is also used for other purposes such as trade negotiations, according to transformation by HST categories, at an agreed level of product classification), of the imported component into the final product; or

2. Value content: The domestic content must be no less than a certain proportion of the value of the final product.[17]

But it is immediately obvious that, even when such common rules are imposed, there are impossible ambiguities in application that lead to chaos. Thus, if Canada imports and also produces steel ingots, how do we decide what imports went into the production of Toyota transplants in Canada? Do we apply the required domestic component

---

17. There can also be some technical requirements for eligibility, such as meeting certain technical standards on safety, but it is obviously rare for such requirements to be imposed differentially against members of the FTA and not against nonmembers.

value to NAFTA, or to Canadian production alone? Even if that were settled, there is the problem that Japanese steel ingots may have used iron ore from the United States and chemicals from Canada; these in turn may have used components from non-NAFTA sources, in an endless regress as one goes back into the product chain. The mind reels as one contemplates the level of ambiguity and the scope for skullduggery and corruption at every stage.

In fact, in the modern age, where multinationals source components from around the world and trade has expanded among many countries, it is a mug's game, and therefore a folly, to run your trade policy on the basis of preferences. Perhaps the most dramatic way the lay person can understand how, in today's world, it is virtually impossible to say which product is whose, is to recall the following witticism about how Princess Diana's death illustrates globalization today:

> An *English* princess with an *Egyptian* boyfriend
> crashes in a *French* tunnel,
> driving a *German* car with a *Dutch* engine
> driven by a *Belgian* who was drunk on *Scottish* whiskey,
> followed closely by *Italian* paparazzi,
> on *Japanese* motorcycles;
> treated by an *American* doctor,
> using *Brazilian* medicines.

> This was sent to us by a *Canadian*,
> using Bill Gates's *American* technology,
> and you're probably reading this on a computer
> that uses *Taiwanese* chips
> and a *Korean* monitor,
> assembled by *Bangladeshi* workers
> in a *Singapore* plant,
> transported by *Indian* lorry-drivers,

hijacked by *Indonesians,*
unloaded by *Sicilian* longshoremen
and trucked to you by *Mexican* illegals.

There are in fact numerous cases where such questions have led to disputes that come for resolution before arbitration and bilateral dispute settlement panels. In a classic case, the U.S. Customs Service refused to certify Hondas produced in Ontario, Canada, as "North American," and hence eligible for duty-free exports from Canada to the United States, on the grounds that, in its own estimation, Canadian Hondas did not meet the local content requirement of more than 50 percent imposed by the Canada-U.S. Free Trade Agreement (CUFTA). Honda countered that its estimates showed that they did. There is no surefire, analytically respectable way to determine the truth in such a case: it all boils down to who has greater stamina and whether Honda is willing to put moneys into legal costs.

But the reality also is far more complex than even this neat but sorry situation. For, in practice, the rules of origin vary between members and nonmembers, across different FTAs by the same country, and across different products within each FTA. For instance, the United States generally applies the substantial transformation test to nonmembers, but, as in the Honda case, it uses the value content test for members of CUFTA and other bilaterals.

Again, in nearly all FTAs worldwide, the rules of origin vary by product. The reason, of course, is that while trade is being freed in these products for imports from member countries, the ability to exploit this opportunity is being undercut by imposing cost-raising rules of origin as required by the specific products. In short, the rules of origin may be described as "made to measure": they vary as necessary to provide an offset to the freeing of trade. They take away with one hand what they give with the other. Christopher Dent has documented that Singapore's FTA with the United States contained "284 pages of product-specific" requirements, and that with Japan had 203 pages.[18]

In fact, the insertion of these extensive product-specific rules of origin, with their deleterious effect on cross-sector uniformity of protection, creates massive treaties that have prompted cynical comments, such as "If NAFTA was really about free trade, you would need only one page, not a document hundreds of pages long." I have seen the NAFTA treaty volume, or I think I have. In some of my debates with the foe of the WTO and free trade Lori Wallach, an articulate and assertive chief of the trade policy division at Ralph Nader's NGO, Public Citizen, she would often carry a fat volume, plonk it down on the table, and announce that it was the NAFTA treaty. Her point was the only one that I wholeheartedly agreed with: that the treaty's bulk reflected the fact that it was freighted with numerous rules of origin and the intrusion of several extraneous issues that had nothing to do with the freeing of trade. I suspect, however, that the NAFTA volume she produced was an empty shell, the way snobbish illiterates fill up their bookshelves with empty book jackets, for otherwise she would get a much-deserved hernia!

The complexity that the spaghetti bowls create for international trade causes distortions in trade and investment. Much energy and many resources must be expended to discover the optimal sourcing of large numbers of components with a view to minimizing the cost of manufacture plus transportation and the differential tariffs and charges levied by origin.[19]

18. See Dent, *New Free Trade Agreements in the Asia-Pacific,* 224.

19. Sometimes the cost of establishing origin is so high for a firm that it decides instead to forgo the process and to pay the MFN tariff. It is not clear how significant this "opting out" is, however.

At a recent meeting in Geneva on PTAs organized by the economist Richard Baldwin, Michael Treschow, the chairman of the board of Ericsson, talked pointedly of the huge difficulties his company faces thanks to the spaghetti bowl. The Hong Kong businessman Victor Fung has written eloquently in the *Financial Times* about the distortions and costs imposed on businesses by the spaghetti bowls:

> Bilateralism distorts the flow of goods, throws up barriers, creates friction, reduces flexibility and raises prices. In structuring the supply chain, every country of origin rule and every bilateral deal has to be tacked on as an additional consideration, thus constraining companies in optimizing production globally. In each new bilateral agreement, considerations relating to "rules of origin" multiply and become more complex. This phenomenon is what trade experts call the "spaghetti bowl effect." While larger companies have a hard time keeping track, for small groups it is impossible. Bilateral agreements cause the business community to work below its potential. In economic terms, bilateral agreements destroy value. If left unchecked, their continued growth has the potential to hinder the development of the global production system.[20]

As Fung notes, these problems and costs created by the spaghetti bowl are particularly onerous for small enterprises. But they are appallingly difficult for the poorer countries, as the former South African trade minister Alex Irwin once stressed to me at Davos. Because of the spaghetti bowl, and because hegemonic powers use PTAs to impose a host of expensive trade-unrelated demands on the poor-country partners in PTAs that reflect lobbying demands in the he-

---

20. Victor Fung, "Bilateral Deals Destroy Global Trade," *Financial Times*, November 3, 2005.

gemon, PTAs are a particularly unattractive trade option for the poor countries relative to multilateralism.

TRADE-UNRELATED ISSUES: TURNING THE TRADE GAME INTO A SHELL GAME

When poor countries enter into PTAs with one another, often under the Enabling Clause, the agreements almost always address trade liberalization. But when they enter into PTAs with hegemonic powers, chiefly the United States and often the European Union, the lobbies in the hegemon countries insist on inserting into the agreements a number of "trade-unrelated" demands on the poor countries. How and why?

First, the lobbies that wish to advance their trade-unrelated agendas by incorporating them into trade treaties and institutions typically mislead by claiming that their agendas are "trade-related." Thus, intellectual property protection has to do with collecting royalties, not with trade. (Of course, almost everything has an *effect* on trade. If I sneeze and use imported cough syrup, that immediately affects imports; if I use domestic cough syrup, that potentially reduces exports of the syrup I have used up. But are we then to include treatment of cough in trade treaties?) By inserting the phrase "trade-related" into the agreement on trade-related intellectual property (TRIPs), the pharmaceutical and software lobbies managed to get the U.S. trade representative at the Uruguay Round to get the issue into the newly formed WTO in 1995. Thanks to this trickery, and use of U.S. political muscle, the WTO became a tripod with three legs: two legitimate ones (the GATT on goods trade and GATS on service trade) and one illegitimate one (TRIPs). The process by which trade-unrelated issues are turned into trade-related matters is a cynical one and an inversion of the truth. In fact, when the phrase "trade-related" is used, you can be sure that the issue is trade-unrelated. It is as if a man who is jilted by his girlfriend goes around saying that he was the one who left her.

Second, it is noteworthy that the PTAs among the poor countries are almost never characterized by the inclusion of such trade-unrelated issues. They concentrate exclusively on trade liberalization. It is only when the hegemonic powers, especially the United States and occasionally the European Union, are involved that one finds the inclusion of such extraneous matters. When important developing countries such as India and Brazil refuse to accommodate these demands and insist on keeping trade negotiations free from such extraneous issues, the reaction is frequently to dismiss these objections as "rejectionist." When President Lula of Brazil refused to extend the proposed Free Trade Agreement of the Americas (FTAA) to include these lobby-driven issues, Washington lobbies and the U.S. trade representative condemned Brazil as embracing an FTAA Lite. (The Andean group of smaller, more compliant nations with little clout and big hunger to sign on to whatever the United States wanted were praised for embracing the "full-blooded" FTAA.) Of course, this linguistic assault in support of a flawed and self-serving position was itself flawed: in an age when everyone is cholesterol conscious, calling a product "Lite" is a compliment, not an insult!

Third, it has become customary to pretend that these trade-unrelated conditions are being imposed "in your interest," that they are really "good for you." Thus, when the software and pharmaceutical industries were advocating intellectual property protection (IPP) during the Uruguay Round, the U.S. trade representative claimed the existence of a study, seen by no one I know, in which benefits had been empirically established for countries moving to adopt

IPP. Not content with such propaganda, U.S. legislators also enacted, as part of the 1988 Omnibus Trade and Competitiveness Act (which I call the Ominous Trade and Competitiveness Act), Section 301 which would legitimate the use of retaliatory tariffs against countries that the United States unilaterally decided were indulging in "unreasonable practices." Part of this legislation was specifically aimed at countries that did not provide intellectual property protection. It was a unilateral measure that had no legitimacy since these countries had not entered into any treaty or even an agreement to adopt such protection.[21]

Finally, the U.S. trade representative made it clear during the negotiations in the Uruguay Round that IPP had to be included in the new WTO if the Uruguay Round was to be concluded. It was a position that all other producers of intellectual property signed on to as in their interest, while pretending publicly that it was also in the interest of the poorer nations themselves, even if they were not producers of intellectual property. Having managed to get TRIPs inserted thus into the WTO, in violation of the fact that royalty collection is not a trade issue, the IPP lobby proceeded to use PTAs to advance their agendas beyond what the multilateral negotiations had yielded. For instance, making no attempt to conceal this objective, U.S. Trade Representative Zoellick notified the U.S. Congress on November 4, 2002, of the administration's intention to negotiate an FTA with the Southern African Customs Union in the following terms: "We plan to use our negotiations with the SACU countries to ... address barriers in

---

21. For an analysis of 301 legislation, and the dangers it posed for the world trading system, see Jagdish Bhagwati and Hugh Patrick, eds., *Aggressive Unilateralism* (Ann Arbor: University of Michigan Press, 1991), especially the chapters by Robert Hudec and by me.

these countries to U.S. exports—including . . . inadequate protection of intellectual property rights." The negotiations were then directed at getting IPP in excess of those agreed to, under de jure and de facto duress in the first instance, at the WTO under the TRIPs agreement. The SACU countries were to be asked to agree on IPP standards "similar to that found in U.S. law" and that exceeded standards agreed to under the TRIPs agreement.[22]

The problem of inclusion of labor and domestic environmental standards in trade treaties is more complex than that relating to matters such as IPP. These are what Robert Hudec and I have called "values-related" demands. They are often demands for harmonization before trade is freed and are often hard to assess and refute because they predispose well-meaning people toward accepting them uncritically.[23] Because these demands are "values-based" (e.g., that workers deserve adequate labor standards), it is also easy to present the hegemonic countries' self-serving demands (motivated by the desire to moderate foreign competition) as if they are really demands made for altruistic reasons aimed at benefiting foreign workers. There are in fact a number of bad arguments for bringing these trade-unrelated issues into

22. See Jonathan Berger and Achal Prabhala, "Assessing the Impact of TRIPs-Plus Rules in the Proposed U.S.-SACU Free Trade Agreement," Working Paper, preliminary draft, Center for Applied Legal Studies, University of Witwatersrand, Johannesburg, South Africa, February 2005.

23. There is a huge literature on this subject, which includes several of my writings in the past fifteen years in places as diverse as the *American Journal of International Law* and two substantial volumes based on a research project involving several of the leading international economists and trade jurists today: Jagdish Bhagwati and Robert Hudec, eds., *Fair Trade and Harmonization: Prerequisites for Free Trade?* (Cambridge, Mass.: MIT Press, 1996). See, in particular, the extensive analytical discussion of the issues involved in Bhagwati and T. N. Srinivasan, "Trade and the Environment: Does Environmental Diversity Detract from the Case for Free Trade?" chapter 4 of Vol. 1.

trade treaties, in one form or another. Such arguments have been floating around for years in the rich-country public domain; they are not compelling and should be rejected.

Take domestic environmental standards (as distinct from international standards, such as to reduce global warming, which involves all nations, or to reduce acid rain, which involves two or more but not all nations).[24] Why does it matter what a producer of steel in Brazil pays by way of a pollution tax for dumping carcinogens in a lake in Brazil that probably no one in the United States has even heard of (especially now that university departments of geography have been increasingly shut down and fewer graduates in the subject are available to teach geography in schools)? Yet if your competitor in Country A pays a lower tax rate than you do, your lobby will insist that this amounts to "unfair trade" and will demand that before trade is freed, Country A must impose an identical burden on your rival.

This sounds reasonable until you spend some time thinking seriously about it. What the pollution tax rate should be (relative to yours) for your foreign rival in your industry cannot be determined except in the total context of the two countries' endowments and preferences. Thus, for instance, even if Mexico and the United States have an identical absolute preference for doing something for the environment, Mexico may have worse water and better air

---

24. International pollution raises a different set of analytical issues than domestic pollution and is usually negotiated in self-standing treaties, such as Kyoto on global warming and the Montreal Protocol on the ozone layer. There are implications for the WTO, for sure, but these have little to do with the question of PTAs versus multilateralism. For instance, see Jagdish Bhagwati and Petros Mavroidis, "Is Action against U.S. Exports for Failure to Sign Kyoto Protocol WTO-Legal?" *World Trade Review* 6, no. 2 (2007): 299–310; and Bhagwati and Srinivasan, "Trade and the Environment: Does Environmental Diversity Detract from the Case for Free Trade?"

than the United States (where many more people drink bottled water or have filters or simply a better water supply, but where there are huge numbers of cars and relatively more polluted air). So it may make perfect sense for Mexico to worry about polluted water and for the United States to worry about polluted air. Correspondingly, it would make perfect sense for Mexico to have higher pollution taxes for industries generating water pollution than the United States does, and for the United States to have higher taxes for industries generating air rather than water pollution. To insist then that what I have called "cross-country intra-industry" pollution taxes be equalized for each industry everywhere is to ignore this elementary piece of logic. Even so, it is the principal driver of demands that domestic environmental standards must be forced via trade treaties and institutions to be identical across countries for the same industry.

When it comes to labor standards, the rationale for legitimate cross-country diversity, reflecting different stages of development and differential economic contexts, is equally pertinent. Generally speaking, countries will have different sequences by which they approach different dimensions of labor standards, as well as different needs and capabilities.[25] For example, the AFL-CIO has insisted on inclusion of labor standards in trade treaties, given its huge concern that competition from the poor countries is hurting U.S.

25. For example, a poor country where workers live in extended families that provide care during postoperative recuperation may not offer medical benefits that extend to the outside provision of home care that may be necessary in countries with only nuclear families. Again, the U.S. standards of safety provisions may be too expensive as a general proposition in India, though they may be necessary for selected, hazardous industries. Some countries, such as France, have considered a 35-hour week to be part of labor rights, although most consider it to be disastrous and France itself is trying to move away from it. In fact, on most dimensions, it is not possible to assert that harmonization across countries makes sense.

workers' wages and threatens their hard-won standards, and bringing foreign countries' labor standards to the level of those in the United States has often been their desire. Yet many have asked: What is so sacrosanct about the labor standards of the United States, where workers' right to strike is badly crippled by half-century-old restrictions, and where the net result has been that union membership has shrunk steadily to almost a tenth of the labor force? It is truly ironic if U.S. labor standards are to be the gold standard for its trading partners.

As it happens, perhaps in response to an appreciation of these and other arguments advanced by scholars who have studied the problem carefully, and the political difficulties of implementing their desire to harmonize the labor standards of poor countries abroad with U.S. practice, the PTA negotiators of the United States with the developing countries initially settled—on the principle of "getting a foot in the door"—for enacting, despite Mexican hesitations, an agreement in an annex to the NAFTA treaty: that each country would enforce its own standards.[26] This agreement was then moved to the main text in the PTAs with Jordan and Morocco. In the case of the PTAs with Peru and Colombia, the U.S. legislators have sought to raise the standards.

In these negotiations, the newly elected Democrats have been the most active, indebted as they are to the financial

---

26. This sounds innocuous but is not. Often, legislation is not expected to be enforced. For that reason, it is often pitched high, with minimum wages, for example, being defined at sumptuous levels that no one expects to pay. Again, laws are left on the books because taking them off would be politically difficult, but no one expects them to be enforced. Thus, there are still laws against adultery in some states, but President Clinton can confidently expect to go to these states without being handcuffed and produced in court because the laws are dormant. Asking developing countries, with their low enforcement ability besides, to enforce their own laws on labor standards is therefore either naïve or cynical.

support and endorsements from the AFL-CIO. They often talk a good game: they say that they want to protect *foreign* workers.[27] Some skeptics make the brutal retort that, if the AFL-CIO really wanted to help foreign workers rather than their American members, they would campaign to relax immigration quotas massively so that the foreign workers would register immediate improvement in their wages and working conditions. But the real problem with the AFL-CIO is that if one reads the campaign speeches of the elected Democrats whom they have supported financially and kept captive to their viewpoints, they move pretty fast from talking about foreign workers' welfare to protesting that competition with workers with lower standards would be tantamount to "unfair" competition and unfair trade. In other words, it all has to do with protecting oneself against foreign rivals. This is why the "old" NAFTA approach of letting the developing countries have, and enforce, their own standards no longer has any political salience: we are back to the demand for "harmonization" of the standards.

Many in the leading developing countries, such as India and Brazil, now see this professed empathy and altruism as masking fear and self-interest. This is also why these countries respond cynically, decrying the hypocrisy of U.S. politicians, which they see as reflected in their claims that what they demand is "in your interest" when it is really in their own interest. In fact, the use of trade treaties to incorporate labor standards is widely seen now as a form of "export protectionism": aimed at raising the cost of production of foreign rivals by forcing on them the same labor standards as in the United States.

---

27. That was also the assertion of presidential candidate Hillary Clinton in a distressing interview with the *Financial Times* printed December 3, 2007.

By now, the tactic has also been diversified into a different demand: that trade treaties require acceptance by all signatories to the core standards of the International Labor Organization (set out in the glossary). It must be noted that these standards are not ratified or adopted as mandatory in most countries, despite frequent citations as if they were. They make for better politics and are aimed at taking the sting out of critics who claim (as above) that the United States is imposing its own standards on others. But does anyone really expect that the United States, which has not ratified many critical ILO conventions, will ratify and follow these conventions or standards? Instead, they will be imposed on the weaker developing countries, amounting in effect to the asymmetrical raising of labor standards that was the original state of play.[28]

But it is pretty clear that, no matter how flawed are the demands to include labor and domestic environmental issues in trade treaties, PTAs with weaker nations offer the best way of getting these demands accepted. And every lobby in Washington, D.C., is playing this game, regardless of the interests of these partner nations themselves. Thus, when the PTAs with Chile and Singapore were being negotiated, the U.S. position was that the use of capital account controls during financial crises ought to be proscribed. This ideological position, favorable to the interests of our financial

---

28. A different interpretation of the AFL–CIO strategy in shifting to ILO standards is that, aside from constituting export protectionism that would help U.S. workers, it can also help the U.S. labor movement itself, as the United States would have to then uphold the ILO core principles. This would be a "backdoor" way of strengthening the hands of the labor movement in the United States. It is doubtful, however, that such an end run around the politics of the country would be consented to by the many, especially Republicans, who consider the labor unions to be inefficient and the AFL–CIO to be their political enemy.

lobbies, was at variance with even the IMF's latest thinking. Chastened by the Asian financial crisis and the successful use of temporary controls on capital flows by Malaysia at the time, the IMF had come around to a more eclectic view of the matter. In the end, the compromise reached by these small nations was that, if controls were instituted and used beyond a stated time period, the financial firms in the United States would be compensated for possible losses. One of my brightest Columbia students had returned to Chile and was on their negotiating team and told me, "Alas, Professor Bhagwati, we are a small country, and we had no option but to fall in line."

Astonishingly, the Australia–U.S. Free Trade Agreement was also witness to lobbying to get Australia's medicine policy, much admired in many circles, changed under pressure from the pharmaceutical lobby in the United States. Entering into force on January 1, 2005, the FTA has been much criticized within Australia. It contains many intellectual property provisions and others related to altering pharmaceutical regulation and public health policy in Australia, as embodied in its Pharmaceutical Benefits Scheme, which had been designed with a view to ensuring equitable and affordable access to essential medicine.[29]

While the PTAs are clearly being used by lobbies in the United States and, to a lesser degree, by the European Union to secure their agendas in one-on-one negotiations with weak nations, one must also entertain the thought that the aim of these lobbies is surely more ambitious. What they

29. Among numerous articles on the subject, I found the following most informative: Thomas Faunce, Evan Doran, David Henry, Peter Drahos, Andrew Searles, Brita Pekarsky, Warwick Neville, and Andrew Searles, "Assessing the Impact of the Australia–United States Free Trade Agreement on Australian and Global Medicines Policy," *Globalization and Health* 15 (2005): 1–10.

cannot secure immediately at the WTO, because the developing countries are there in greater numbers and can resist the pressure from the hegemonic powers by the sheer force of their numbers and some ability and willingness to take concerted stands in their own interest, the hegemonic powers can hope to secure by breaking away the developing countries one by one through the PTAs. Thus, if a developing country has signed a PTA with the United States that includes labor standards provisions, that country is unlikely to say at the WTO: We will not have labor standards at the WTO. This is in fact a strategy of "divide and conquer." The United States can be interpreted as playing this strategic game, hoping to get its lobbies' agendas on to the WTO by using the PTAs as a mechanism by which the opposition to these lobbies' agendas is steadily eroded at the WTO. Charles Kindleberger wrote about "altruistic hegemons" providing leadership for the world trading system; here we have the strategic behavior of what I have called a "selfish hegemon."[30]

ARE PTAS BUILDING BLOCKS OR STUMBLING BLOCKS TO MULTILATERAL FREE TRADE?

Recall that the original embrace of PTAs by the United States in the early 1980s was a result of frustration with the inability to get multilateral talks started under GATT auspices. Once the Uruguay Round was launched, the United States should have reverted to its traditional "multilateralism only" doctrine that it adhered to for over 30 years. But it did not. In fact, its leadership, mainly Secretary of State Baker and his deputy,

---

30. The phrase and idea of a "selfish hegemon" was introduced by me in "Threats to the World Trading System: Income Distribution and the Selfish Hegemon," *Journal of International Affairs* 48 (1994): 279–285.

Robert Zoellick, decided that the United States should do both. Their argument was that PTAs would, in terminology that I introduced, serve as "building blocks" toward multi-lateral freeing of trade, that the two trade policies were complementary, that they were "friends," not "foes." They would soon call it the theory of "competitive liberalization." As Zoellick put it eloquently in 2003:

> When the Bush administration set out to revitalize America's trade agenda almost three years ago, we outlined our plans clearly and openly: We would pursue a strategy of "competitive liberalization" to advance free trade globally, regionally, and bilaterally. By moving forward simultaneously on multiple fronts the United States can overcome or bypass obstacles; exert maximum leverage for openness, *target the needs of developing countries,* especially the most committed to economic and political reforms; establish models of success, especially in cutting-edge areas; strengthen America's ties with all regions within a global economy; and create a fresh political dynamic by putting free trade on the offensive.[31]

Zoellick thus argued that the United States would use the FTAs to advance a number of trade-unrelated objectives, and (astonishingly) that these issues were in fact addressing the "needs of developing countries," when in fact (as discussed earlier) they were being imposed by the United States

31. Cited in Evenett and Meier, "An Interim Assessment of the U.S. Trade Policy of 'Competitive Liberalization,'" emphasis added. It is from a report by the U.S. General Accounting Office on international trade, January 2004. Other such pronouncements by Zoellick are on record as well. Perhaps the most remarkable one is from Zoellick's Op Ed piece, "Our Credo: Free Trade and Competition," *Wall Street Journal,* July 10, 2003: "FTAs break new ground— they establish prototypes for liberalization in areas such as services, e-commerce, intellectual property for knowledge societies, transparency in government regulation, and better enforcement of labor and environmental protections."

as a precondition to signing an FTA with it. In addition, Zoellick and his U.S. trade representative deputies also claimed that such initiatives would prompt other countries to seek trade liberalization, first in the shape of FTAs with the United States, and second, by embracing the multilateral system and negotiations at the WTO.

The former is surely an exaggerated claim, at best. While preferences are a wasting asset as MFN tariffs come down over time, the willingness of the United States to sign more FTAs implies that the preferences earned by signing an FTA with the United States are also a wasting asset, insofar as your close rivals may also join an FTA. Simon Evenett and Michael Meier in fact find far too few public statements by policy makers worldwide to the effect that they would like an FTA with the United States because their rivals have one.[32]

The fact that the United States uses threats to force countries into FTAs also makes one skeptical that countries are rushing to sign on just because others have. Thus, during the critical referendum on the Central America Free Trade Agreement (CAFTA) in Colombia, where the opposition was considerable despite governmental support for it, the U.S. trade representative issued a strong warning that Costa Rica would lose its GSP one-way preferences if CAFTA was not approved, that is, that the failure to vote for CAFTA would imply that Costa Rica's existing market access would be reduced! So instead of Costa Rica's main motivation for joining CAFTA being better market access, its losing market access to the United States if it did not join became the issue. Similar threats have been used against other countries. For

---

32. Perhaps the most dramatic such statements are from New Zealand vis-à-vis the Australia-U.S. FTA and the plaintive worries of Colombia, struggling to get its FTA with the United States, over the fact that Peru has gotten ahead in the queue.

instance, with the Andean Trade Preferences Act expiring in February 2008, the United States has insisted that Peru and Colombia sign on to FTAs with the United States or lose preferences, leaving the two countries with a Hobson's choice: join the FTA on our terms or face increased barriers.[33]

In fact, Arvind Panagariya has reminded me that, because one-way preferences granted by the EU and the United States to many developing countries expired in 2007, these countries are at risk of having to sign on to FTAs, often with onerous conditions, if their market access is not going to suffer. The number of such countries is large. The EU alone maintains one-way preferences for as many as 71 countries spread over Africa, the Caribbean, and Pacific (ACP) regions. Originally granted under Lome Convention I (1975–80), these preferences were continued under Lome II–IV (1980–2000) and most recently, in 2001, under the Cotonou Agreement (2001–7). These trade preferences cover 99 percent of the industrial products of ACP countries without quantitative limits and are superior to the GSP scheme offered to all developing countries.[34] The new, reciprocal "economic partnership agreements," in effect PTAs, being offered in place of the expiring one-way preferences have led to objections from countries such as South Africa and Namibia, who have refused to accept conditions that detract from their sovereignty in unacceptable ways.[35]

33. In fact, the United States also used threats to force Colombia off the G-20 group that had materialized at the Cancun meeting in 2003. See the excellent paper by Craig Van Grasstek, "Asia Pacific Regional Initiative on Trade, Economic Governance, and Human Development," unpublished manuscript, Kennedy School of Government, Harvard University, June 2004.

34. See Arvind Panagariya, "EU Preferential Trade Agreements and Developing Countries," *World Economy* 25, no. 10 (2002): 1415–32.

35. See "Two African Nations Refuse to Join EU Trade Deal," *Financial Times,* December 3, 2007.

Nor should we rule out the fact that, as explained in chapter 2, a non-negligible fraction of the FTAs with the United States have been dictated principally by security reasons rather than by "competitive liberalization." Among these are FTAs with Singapore, Jordan, Morocco, and now the pending FTA with South Korea. Moreover, in defiance of U.S. hegemony, countries in other regions have signed "tit-for-tat" FTAs (especially in Asia) that exclude the United States just as the United States has excluded countries in other regions from NAFTA and its plans for the FTAA.

The other claim by the U.S. trade representative, that its FTAs also advance WTO negotiations, is even more problematic. Fred Bergsten, a prominent trade expert in Washington, D.C., is a leading exponent of this view. His principal claim of a positive link between PTAs and multilateral trade negotiations is the assertion that the Uruguay Round was brought to a close because the APEC Summit in Seattle in November 1993 was used by the United States to threaten the recalcitrant European Union that if the EU did not close the Round, the United States would have a competing alternative: APEC liberalization. I have asked many European trade officials about his claim, and they simply laugh at it. I got the same reaction from the *Financial Times* trade correspondent Guy de Jonquieres, with whom I discussed this assertion in Cebu, Philippines, in August 2006, when I gave the keynote address to ABAC, the business advisory arm of APEC. The spaghetti bowl of Asian FTAs was a central theme of discussion, prompting Jonquieres to write a column on the subject. He found no evidence for Bergsten's assertion either. Surely, everyone could see that there was not the slightest chance that APEC, with its many disparate economies and political differences, would turn into an FTA. In fact, for years afterward, the Article 24 model was rejected despite U.S. objections; the approach adopted, under mainly Australian and Japanese leadership, was one of "concerted unilateral liberalization" which would be undertaken on an MFN basis. Bergsten's contention would therefore require us to believe that the Europeans were a bunch of nitwits! Besides, Bergsten's view assumes, happily for Washington, that the main obstacle to concluding the Uruguay Round was the European Union, not the United States.

The implausibility of the benign Bergsten argument leaves one with a whole range of arguments that suggest instead that the effect of PTAs on the multilateral trade negotiations is malign. Take just six of the most plausible concerns:[36]

1. Consider that a dollar's worth of lobbying on opening up Mexico under a PTA will get the Mexican market opened to you. But if you spend the same dollar in Geneva, opening up the Mexican market on an MFN basis, your benefit will be diluted by the "free riders," your rivals from EU, Japan, and elsewhere who have not spent any money to open the Mexican market. So you will spend the dollar on PTAs, not on MTN.

2. Although there are any number of routine bureaucrats available to negotiate trade deals, the supply of skilled bureaucrats is always limited. If PTAs are being pursued simultaneously with MTN, you can be sure that the talented bureaucrats' attention will be split, at best. I saw this in Seattle in November 1999 when the WTO meeting erupted under protests. U.S. Trade Representative Charlene Barshefsky arrived just in time, after long trade negotiations with China: her eye was not on the WTO ball.

---

36. For a more theoretical way of considering the link between PTAs and MTN, or what theorists now call the "dynamic time-path" question, see the appendix on the current state of research on these questions. Apropos these theoretical formulations and relevant empirical evidence, however, see also the next footnote.

3. Politicians often equate all kinds of trade deals, so if you nail down a PTA, no matter how negligible in trade volume, that is a feather in your cap. In fact, I was once at a Bureau of Labor function to honor a bureaucrat whom U.S. Trade Representative Mickey Kantor congratulated for participating in negotiations of over 250 trade deals. Of these, one was the Uruguay Round, another was NAFTA (much less important and, in fact, arguably even a mistake), and the rest were trade-restricting, quota-setting textiles deals under the Multi-Fiber Arrangement!

4. Lobbies provide the foot soldiers in the battles to open trade, and I have already documented that several lobbies with trade-unrelated causes also find PTAs, where weak countries can be intimidated into making concessions, a more agreeable way to go. These lobbies use the PTAs to provide templates—"Ah, we now have our agenda accepted as a part of trade liberalization, and that is the way it will be for other PTAs from now on"—and to steadily encircle the WTO to push their agendas. Aside from the AFL-CIO, few groups are spending as much time and money on Doha as on the PTAs with Peru and Colombia.

5. In the United States, given the general anxiety over trade, it has been a mistake to ask politicians (especially Democrats who have unions among their constituents) to repeatedly spend their limited pro-trade political capital on a succession of trivial PTAs, leading to "trade fatigue" that afflicts then the Doha Round as well.

6. Finally, recent empirical analysis by Nuno Limao, using tariff reduction data during the most recent MTN, demonstrates that PTAs by the United States were a stumbling block to multilateral trade liberalization.[37] The adverse effect operates through the

37. Nuno Limao, "Preferential Trade Agreements as Stumbling Blocks for Multilateral Trade Liberalization: Evidence for the U.S., *American Economic Review* 96, no. 3 (June 2006), 896–914. This paper's brilliant empirical analysis nicely complements the theoretical analyses such as those of Phil Levy and Pravin Krishna, reviewed in the appendix, on the question of the dynamic time-path issues concerning PTAs.

mechanism that the hegemon maintains higher multilateral tariffs on products imported from the preferential trade partner relative to those on similar products imported from the rest of the world. These higher MFN tariffs act virtually as bargaining chips to be used in negotiating PTAs, because the value of the preference increases the higher the MFN tariff is. This provides an incentive not to reduce MFN tariffs relative to the situation where PTAS were not permitted.

It is hard indeed to contemplate the consequences of PTAs with equanimity. The most important item on our policy agenda has to be to devise an appropriate response to their spread and the damage they impose on the multilateral trading system.

CHAPTER 4

What Do We Do Now?

Evidently, the problems raised by the PTA proliferation are now much understood. With politicians and governments worldwide in the throes of this pandemic—and unable or unwilling to grasp the difficult lesson that doing nothing is preferable to proliferating PTAs that are seriously damaging the multilateral world trading system—several directors general of the GATT and the WTO have shown keen awareness of the problems and expressed varying degrees of alarm, chief among them, Arthur Dunkel, Supachai Panitchpakdi, Peter Sutherland, and Pascal Lamy.[1] Clearly, the situation regarding PTAs cries out for palliatives and for solutions.

Three options have been explored: (1) halting the formation of new PTAs and eliminating the preferences in existing PTAs through built-in reductions of the differentials between MFN tariffs on nonmembers and the preferential tariffs on members; (2) reducing the chaos of the spaghetti

---

1. See my discussion of their role in the preface.

Arthur Dunkel was the director general of the GATT between January 1980 and June 1993. He is widely credited with having overseen the Uruguay Round, nurturing it through many vicissitudes and saving it from collapse. A staunch proponent of multilateralism, he was concerned with PTAs enough to commission a special study of these proliferating threats to multilateralism toward the end of his last term in office. *WTO.*

bowl through harmonization and similar techniques that turn the spaghetti, as it were, into lasagna; and (3) using multilateral trade negotiations such as the Doha Round to reduce the MFN tariffs to negligible levels, thus reducing the preference by indirection: preferences relative to zero would be zero. The first two are well-meaning palliatives that require addressing the PTAs themselves directly; for this reason, their practicality is limited. The last measure, on the other hand, seeks instead to redress by indirection the problem posed by PTAs and requires no amendment of existing PTAs or prohibition of new ones, offering to eliminate not the preferences themselves but their efficacy. It is therefore the solution that offers the greatest promise.

PROPOSALS TO ELIMINATE THE PREFERENCES AT SOURCE

Halting the formation of PTAs is no longer a possibility. When the Uruguay Round was launched, there was a distinct possibility, as I have argued, that the United States could have exercised its huge weight in the trading system and as a political superpower to tell the European Union that resort to Article 24 had to be proscribed, or else the United States would retaliate on other fronts. Instead, the United States joined in, which then led Asia also to abandon its principled opposition to PTAs.

A pause in considering new PTAs by the EU was also short-lived as European businessmen reportedly cited in turn the growing U.S. FTAs as a reason why the EU should resume its own FTAs. Otherwise, they warned, European business would suffer. In turn, the argument that the EU would forge ahead on its bilaterals had fueled the U.S. pursuit of FTAs. Now, many governments talk about "not falling behind," and (as I explained in chapter 2) they occasionally argue that "everyone is doing it." The genie, and not a benign one, is out of the bottle.

But then there are proposals to reduce the external tariffs of FTA members so as to be closer to the internal intra-member tariffs, steadily reducing the gap between the MFN tariffs and the internal tariffs. This proposal for "radioactive reduction" of the preference granted to PTA members has not gone anywhere, however: few PTA members would want to have the preferences they enjoy to be eroded thus.

Dr. Supachai Panitchpakdi, director general of the WTO (2002–5) in a divided term with Michael Moore of New Zealand, was the deputy prime minister of Thailand and was quick to understand the problems posed by PTAs. The consultative group of experts that he appointed to look into the future of the WTO, under the chairmanship of Peter Sutherland, was encouraged by him to include an analysis of proliferating preferences, resulting in chapter 2 of the eventual report (2005), and played a major role in prompting worldwide discussion of the problems they pose. *UNCTAD*.

TURNING SPAGHETTI INTO LASAGNA (AND THEN INTO PIZZA)

If PTAs cannot be halted or amended so as to make preferences subject to built-in demise on schedule, can we still build a scenario in which at least the current chaos of the spaghetti bowl is minimized by coordinated action to harmonize rules of origin, for instance?

To put it another way, can we argue plausibly that the many bilateral PTAs, despite their immediate impact in creating systemic undermining of nondiscrimination in the trading system, can nonetheless be seen as building blocks for multilateralism, that they could all be aggregated into plurilateral regional groups that, in turn, would be further aggregated in the next step to take us to the Holy Grail of

Pascal Lamy is the current director general of the WTO, from September 2005. A French socialist, he has been an important supporter of free trade and was the commissioner for trade in the European Union. Noted for not having started any new PTAs while he was in charge of the EC portfolio, he has taken the lead at the WTO on addressing frontally the issues raised by PTAs. *WTO.*

substantially freed multilateral trade? This, in fact, was asserted by many commentators in the late 1980s and early 1990s. Perhaps the chief proponent of this view was Lester Thurow, who famously declared in 1988 in Davos, "GATT is dead," prompting me to retort that, with so many nations lined up to join GATT, necrophilia must have broken out! But endorsing the shift to preferential trade agreements as the way to go was thought to provide a path to multilateral free trade, a favored scenario being that the three major hegemons—the United States, the European Union, and Japan—would bring together into regional FTA grouping the countries in their sphere of influence. The United States would slap together the countries in South America, the EU would pull together Africa, and Japan would do the same for Asia.

It was a romantic and politically naïve idea, ignoring the fact that some South Americans resent the Yankees, some Africans are skeptical about entering into a deep embrace of the metropolitan powers in Europe that had penetrated Africa and colonized it, and the Asian nations have tragic memories of Japan in World War II. Indeed, as preferential trade agreements multiplied, the regional groupings, driven by different politics, cut across this enticing triptych; for instance, APEC has members drawn from both South America and Asia.

But collapsing the bilateral FTAs into regional groups raises not just political but nearly insuperable "technical" difficulties. To see this, take a metaphor used by Koichi Hamada, arguably Japan's most distinguished economist today. Drawing on the spaghetti bowl metaphor, he wittily remarked that the spaghetti could turn into lasagna: spaghetti or noodles (the bilaterals) could turn into lasagnas (subregional or regional FTAs), which in turn could merge into the giant-size pizza of fully multilateral trade.

Now, even lasagnas, like spaghetti, are not all identical.[2] So adding together the Tuscan lasagna with béchamel sauce, the Ligurian with pesto sauce, and the Neapolitan with ricotta is unlikely to work, any more than, to revert to the metaphor of building and stumbling blocks, one can make the multilateral mansion with bilateral bricks of different shapes and sizes. But the difficulty with Hamada's intriguing suggestion is even more fundamental. Lasagna cannot be

---

2. Spaghetti, like noodles, comes in different shapes and sizes, of course, as anyone ordering it in a fine Italian restaurant knows.

made from spaghetti: it needs flat pasta. And pizza cannot be made from lasagna either!

This becomes evident when one looks at the different FTAs in depth. First, the tariff rates applied to specific products are very different across FTAs; getting a large number of them to "merge" would require reconciling these differences. This is true enough when we are trying to eliminate tariff differences among PTAs enacted under Article 24. But imagine doing this when there are many negotiated under the Enabling Clause, where tariff reductions can be partial, confined to a few sectors, and therefore chaotically different for the same items across different PTAs.

Product-specific rules of origin would also vary across FTAs by product; designed with a view to restraining competition resulting from the freeing of trade, they would raise equally difficult problems. Even if magically one Rule of Origin was technically agreed upon—it has not yet been—would the lobbies that have negotiated a plethora of rules of origin to arrive at their preferred "political equilibrium" suddenly abandon them just because we want to turn the spaghetti into lasagna?

In addition, recall that the PTAs negotiated by the United States have increasingly been used by lobbies with trade-unrelated agendas to insert their demands into the PTAs. Thus, the United States now introduces labor and environmental issues into bilaterals, and also restrictions on use of capital controls and enhanced agreements on intellectual property protection that go well beyond what the TRIPs agreement at the WTO requires. With bilateral PTAs negotiated with different requirements by the United States over the past 20 years, there is a lot of diversity, which makes collapsing the PTAs into one unified format difficult. Moreover, even if the three "regional" lasagnas were magically to materialize, how could they possibly merge into the multilateral pizza when each of the three has different menus of trade-unrelated demands?

Nonetheless, one finds unrealistic statements from time to time by political leaders, especially those who are busy proliferating PTAs, expressing the hope that somehow the spaghetti can be turned into lasagna. Thus Prime Minister Goh Chok Tong of Singapore, which has signed several FTAs, expressed the hope in 2001 that "[Singapore's] FTAs actually will pave the way for APEC-wide trade area," and that it was "Singapore's intention to spin a web of interlocking free trade agreements between APEC members, which could help move the organization toward achieving free trade in the Asia-Pacific."[3] This is a remarkable triumph of hope against reality, if a "regionwide" FTA is intended rather than just a talking shop, since the nations involved would include the United States, China, and Japan.

Such unrealistic expressions of hope are widespread, perhaps indicating unease with the increased realization by these politicians that their pursuit of PTAs has pernicious and perverse effects. Thus President Ricardo Lagos of Chile, speaking as the host of the 2004 APEC Summit, said, "What happens if you put together all the agreements that already exist among the different APEC economies? If you put all those agreements together, then it may emerge probably—a general kind of agreement among the different countries."[4] One may rest assured that President Lagos has never seen an FTA agreement, any more than most of us have.

<hr />

3. Quoted in Dent, *New Free Trade Agreements in Asia-Pacific*, 227. Also see the excellent article by him, "Full Circle? Ideas and Ordeals of Creating a Free Trade Area of the Asia-Pacific," *Pacific Review* 20, no. 4 (2007), 447–74, highlighting the immense, almost insuperable, difficulties of going from spaghetti to lasagna.

4. Quoted in Dent, *New Free Trade Agreements in Asia-Pacific*, 228.

Admittedly, these problems arise acutely in regard to the existing flood of PTAs. One could try to impose certain rules that every new PTA must follow: in particular, choice of one Rule of Origin for all products, only one set of trade-unrelated demands, identical tariffs on each commodity across different PTAs. But does anyone imagine that this could be done worldwide, or even within one broad region? The most that has been done recently is in regard to what are known as "cumulation rules": if there are several PTAs by the United States, the content requirements that may be used for the preference to apply to a product by a member country of any of these PTAs are interpreted to include intermediates or raw materials imported from members of all of the PTAs in question.[5] But frankly, this amounts to very little. The most critical problems still remain.

BRINGING THE MFN TARIFFS DOWN TO NEGLIGIBLE LEVELS

In the end, one partial and indirect solution remains. Preferences are relative to the MFN tariff. So if we cannot do much about the PTAs directly to remove the preference, we can virtually eliminate PTAs by reducing the MFN tariff itself to zero. That is, because we are dealing with a ratio, if we can do nothing about the numerator, we can work on the denominator to get the ratio down to what we want. Of course, not everyone understands ratios. Beryl Sprinkel, chair of the Council of Economic Advisers to President Reagan, is reputed to have said in exasperation with the European demands over the dollar: Let them look after their

5. Sometimes cumulation rules, or their variants, are applied politically. Thus the U.S.-Jordan FTA explicitly encourages Israeli content in Jordanian products.

exchange rate and we will look after ours. It makes a splendid examination question in international macroeconomics.

As the PTA pandemic escalates, many now feel that the cure is to progressively reduce the MFN tariffs. Therefore, insofar as the MFN tariffs are more likely to be cut under reciprocity than through unilateral liberalization, we cannot afford to have the Doha Round fail. Nor, as we settle it (which we will), can we afford not to go on to the next round.

I must admit that this indirect solution addresses only the damage done by PTAs to the trading system through tariff preferences. But as I noted in chapter 3, the downside of PTAs for the developing countries in particular has included the capture by the lobbies of the hegemonic powers (principally the United States but increasingly the European Union as well) to impose trade-unrelated agendas, which have no demonstrable advantage and, in fact, clear disadvantages for the developing countries. It is time for these countries to wake up to what is going on as they are bamboozled into accepting onerous trade-unrelated demands as the permanent price for preferences whose effectiveness steadily erodes as they are extended to others and as MFN declines, however slowly. The Scandinavians have long argued that just because assistance is called aid, it does not amount to aid; that a gift horse may be a Trojan horse. It is time for the developing countries to extend the Scandinavian warning of caveat emptor to the trade arena.

I am happy that the larger developing countries have drawn a line in the sand on including trade-unrelated agendas in their PTAs with the hegemonic powers. Last year India firmly told the EU to drop its trade-unrelated demands if it wanted an FTA with India, and, as I noted in the previous chapter, Brazil under President Lula also has remained firm on rejecting such demands under the U.S.-proposed FTAA. These are large countries, with democratic systems, and they have sufficient self-respect not to be bullied by the hegemonic powers into supine acceptance of unjustifiable demands masked by false smiles and fulsome and fleeting praise. Some developing-country intellectuals have even suggested that PTAs be signed with important developed countries such as Japan, which sticks to trade issues in PTAs, so as to provide an alternative template that excludes such demands.

Indeed, some of the third-world NGOs are also waking up to this threat. There is evidence that instead of militating against trade and fulminating against populist, ill-informed, and ill-argued claims of "unfair trade,"[6] they are increasingly turning their focus to the way the hegemonic powers are using the trade agenda to advance their lobbies' agendas to the detriment of the poor countries. They need all the support of the governments of the developing countries in this contest, especially as some of the powerful NGOs in the First World who support one or more of these lobbying demands have vastly greater moneys and are besides financed by their own governments to advance these very same trade-unrelated agendas. Only a realistic appreciation of the way the PTA trade game is played, the threat it poses to the WTO itself through the policy of "divide and conquer" at the WTO, and the mobilization of intellectuals and econ-omists who see through the game of the hegemonic powers and their lobbies can provide the countervailing power that

---

6. "Fair trade" is a populist slogan, embraced and propagated by Oxfam, whose expertise does not match its increasing outreach that ambitiously goes into issues beyond famines and disaster relief, and by ill-informed economists like my distinguished colleague Joe Stiglitz, who also has little expertise in international trade. Unfortunately, even a cursory acquaintance with international trade policy shows that "fair trade" is the slogan used by protectionists to stop the freeing of trade restrictions applied to developing countries; its propagation is a surefire recipe for slowing down the freeing of trade for these countries and also for giving a superficially appealing rationale for the imposition of trade-unrelated agendas on them.

the situation calls for. This will be an uphill battle, as the political ability of hegemonic powers and the financial power of their well-endowed lobbies make a formidable combination to go up against.[7]

The solution of pursuing MFN trade liberalization to reduce the effect of preferences is less problematic. Nonetheless, one has to confront the fact that, as I noted in the previous chapter, while the need to have multilateral negotiations succeed is the greater with the PTAs proliferating, the ability to do so politically may have been damaged. It will require considerable political leadership and will to surmount that difficulty. But surmount it we must.

7. As Mr. Zoellick is a principal architect of the PTAs policy in the United States and was the most articulate supporter of the embrace of these trade-unrelated agendas when he was U.S. trade representative, his elevation to the Presidency of the World Bank by the U.S. administration requires attention. Unfortunately, the World Bank is a donor institution, and its leadership can wind up playing for hegemonic interests by helping to nudge the client states for the World Bank's largesse into a "prudent" acceptance of the PTAs and the trade-unrelated agendas that the U.S. administration continues to propagate.

The Theory of Preferential Trade Agreements: Historical Evolution and Current Trends

The theory of preferential trade agreements (PTAs) has undergone two phases of evolution, in two very different modes, largely reflecting the contrasting policy concerns of the time. In this appendix, I trace this evolution, offering both a historical context and an intellectual coherence to diverse analytical approaches.[1]

STATIC ANALYSIS: TRADE CREATION AND TRADE DIVERSION

Viner: Cutting Tariffs Preferentially

It is well known that Jacob Viner (1950) pioneered the static analysis of PTAs. His analysis was prompted by policy concerns about PTAs, tracing from the Havana Charter for the aborted International Trade Organization. The formation

---

1. This appendix provides an accessible guide to the major developments in the theory of PTAs in the postwar period. It complements and completes for the

of the European Community in 1957, and of the European Free Trade Agreement, gave a more direct policy dimension to this theory and led to important analytical insights, especially from the work in the 1950s of Richard Lipsey and Kelvin Lancaster, Harry Johnson, and James Meade.

The essential message of the Vinerian approach, as explained in the text, was that PTAs, as distinct from nondiscriminatory trade liberalization, could harm both a member country and world welfare. PTAs could be either "trade diverting" or "trade creating." These Vinerian concepts have been reworked by many, but the essential point remains an important contribution.[2]

Kemp-Wan-Ohyama: Necessarily Welfare-Improving Customs Unions

Although the Vinerian approach has proved to be the most potent in theory and in policy thinking, it violated the lay person's view, which may now be corrupting the policy domain, that PTAs are a good thing because they are a move toward free trade. The beauty of the influential 1976 paper by Murray C. Kemp and Henry Wan, whose basic insight was anticipated by Kemp (1964) and Vanek (1965), leading to an obscure contribution by Michihiro Ohyama (1972), was to show that one could always construct a welfare-

---

reader the policy-related analysis of PTAs that the text principally provides. It is based on a short survey of the subject in Jagdish Bhagwati and Arvind Panagariya, "The Theory of Preferential Trade Agreements: Historical Evolution and Current Trends," *American Economic Review*, Papers and proceedings, May 1996.

    2. See, in particular, the discussion in the text of the suggestion that trade diversion may be minimized if PTAs are formed among "natural trading partners," drawing on Paul Wonnacott and Mark Lutz (1989), Lawrence Summers (1991), Paul Krugman (1991), Jeffrey Frankel, Ernesto Stein, and Shang-Lin Wei (1995), Panagariya (1995), and Bhagwati and Panagariya (1996).

improving CU among any subset of countries, while the nonmembers were left at their initial welfare. The Kemp-Wan demonstration, however, is really a "possibility theorem." Recently, economists such as Christopher Bliss (1994) and T. N. Srinivasan (1997) have begun to give structure to the analysis; Srinivasan, for example, proceeds to compare the Kemp-Wan tariff, under alternative models, to the Article 24 requirement that the common external tariff of a CU should, on average, be unchanged.

Cooper-Massell-Johnson-Bhagwati: Customs Unions to Minimize Cost of Industrialization

After the Treaty of Rome, many developing countries sought (unsuccessfully, in the end) to form similar FTAs or CUs on the grounds that, given the protection against the industrialized North, they could liberalize among themselves and reduce the cost of their industrialization, an idea that was developed independently in C. A. Cooper and B. F. Massell (1965), Harry Johnson (1965), and Bhagwati (1968).

Only recently has a proper proof of this proposition been provided by Pravin Krishna and Bhagwati (1994), who saw that the argument could be proved simply as a version of the Kemp-Wan theorem, with an added policy instrument thrown in to achieve the targeted degree of member-country industrialization.

Brecher-Bhagwati: Member-Country-Welfare Effect of Policy and Parametric Changes in a Common Market

Alternatively, the case where there is a common market, with full factor mobility, has been analyzed by Richard Brecher and Bhagwati (1981). That paper also considers how changes, such as in the external tariff, in technical know-how, or in capital accumulation, affect the welfare of individual countries. This analysis is clearly relevant to analysis of policy questions such as the effect of a change in the Common Agricultural Policy on, say, British welfare.

Grossman-Helpman-Krishna: The Political Economy Theoretic Analysis of PTA Formation

Finally, with the recent interest in the theory of political economy and the desire to analyze why PTAs are becoming popular, the cutting-edge theory of PTAs has moved into modeling the incentives to form PTAs. The chief insight of Gene Grossman and Elhanan Helpman (1995) and of Krishna (1998) is to show how trade diversion provides a principal motive for forming such PTAs. In addition, the political economy analysis of PTAs has been extended to other questions. Thus, Panagariya and Ronald Findlay (1996) have shown that reduced protection in an FTA can lead to incentives to raise tariffs on nonmember countries—an important policy issue because such raising of barriers is possible with administered protection.

DYNAMIC TIME-PATH ANALYSIS: BUILDING BLOCKS VERSUS STUMBLING BLOCKS

In contrast to the question of whether the immediate (static) effect of an FTA is good, we may ask whether the (dynamic time-path) effect of the FTA is to accelerate or decelerate the continued reduction of trade barriers toward the goal of reducing them worldwide.

We now have the key concepts in the dynamic time-path case of PTAs acting as "stumbling blocks" or "building blocks" toward worldwide nondiscriminatory trade liberalization, introduced by Bhagwati (1991), just as Viner (1950) introduced the key concepts of trade diversion and trade creation for the static analysis.

Formulating the Dynamic Time-Path Question

The time-path question may be formulated analytically in two separate ways.

Analytical Question I. Assume that the time-path of multi-lateral trade negotiations (MTN) and the time-path of PTAs are separable and do not influence each other, so that neither hurts nor helps the other. Will the PTA time-path be characterized by stagnant or negligible expansion of membership, or will there be expanding membership, with this even turning eventually into worldwide membership, as in the WTO, thus arriving at nondiscriminatory free trade for all? The analysis can be extended to a comparison of the two time-paths, ranking the efficacy of the two methods of reducing trade barriers to achieve the goal of worldwide free trade for all.

Analytical Question II. Assume instead, as is plausible, that if both the MTN and the PTA time-paths are embraced simultaneously, they will interact. In particular, the policy of undertaking PTAs will have a malign or a benign impact on the progress along the MTN time-path.

Question I can be illustrated with the aid of Figure A.1, which portrays a sample of possibilities for the time-paths. World welfare is put on the vertical axis, and time is put on the horizontal axis. For the PTA time-paths drawn, an upward movement along the path implies growing membership; for the MTN time-paths, it implies nondiscriminatory lowering of trade barriers among the nearly worldwide WTO membership. The PTA and MTN time-paths are assumed to be independent of each other, not allowing for the PTA time-path to either accelerate or

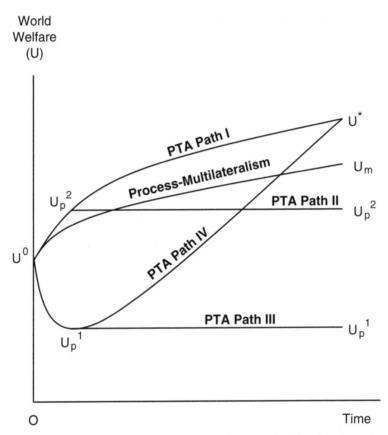

FIGURE A.1. Illustration of the concepts of PTAs as building blocks and stumbling blocks for nondiscriminatory trade liberalization.

Note: The PTAs may improve welfare immediately from U^0 to U_p^2 or (because of net trade diversion) reduce it to U_p^1. The time-path with FTAs, in either case, could be stagnant (paths II and III), implying a fragmentation of the world economy through no further expansion of the initial trade block; or it could lead (paths I and IV) to multilateral free trade for all at U^* through continued expansion and coagulation of PTAs. Under process-multilateralism, the time-path may fail to reach U^* and instead fall short at U_m because of free-rider problems; or it may overcome them and reach U^*. This diagram assumes that the time-paths are independent, so that embarking on a PTA path does not affect the process-multilateralism path. The text, however, discusses such interdependence.

Source: Adapted from Bhagwati [1993].

decelerate the course of MTN (thus ruling out the type of issues in Question II). The goal can be treated as reaching U*, the worldwide freeing of trade barriers on a nondiscriminatory basis, at a specified time.

Question I can then be illustrated by reference to the PTA paths I–IV. Thus, PTAs may improve welfare immediately, in the static sense, or reduce it. In either case, the time-path could then be stagnant (as with time-paths II and III), implying a fragmentation of the world economy through no further expansion of the initial PTA. Alternatively, it can lead (as in time-paths I and IV) to multilateral free trade for all at U* through continued expansion and coalescence of the PTAs. Under "process multilateralism" (i.e., MTN as a multilateral process of reducing trade barriers, as distinct from multilateralism as the goal desired), the time-path may fail to reach U* and instead fall short at U_m because of free-rider problems. As indicated, if the PTA and MTN time-paths are interdependent, we can address Question II. In that case, the MTN time-path becomes a function of whether the PTA time-path is traveled simultaneously. The dynamic time-path question has arisen, just as the static one did, in policy concerns and political decisions that ran ahead of the theory. It arose in the context of the U.S. failure to get an MTN round started at the GATT in 1982 and the U.S. decision finally to abandon its avoidance of GATT Article 24-sanctioned PTAs. This was a Hobson's choice: if the MTN could not be used to continue lowering trade barriers, then PTAs would need to be used instead.

But, as discussed in the text, the United States has wound up becoming committed to "walking on both legs," embracing both the PTA and the MTN paths, and its spokesmen have implied that PTAs will have a beneficial impact through induced acceleration of MTN. The questions distinguished above spring therefore from this shift in U.S. policy. In Bhagwati (1991, 1993), the challenge to international trade theorists (to analyze these questions) was first identified and a preliminary set of arguments offered. I now systematize the theoretical literature that has developed subsequently.

"Exogenously Determined" Time-Paths: A Diversion

First, consider theoretical approaches that are not meaningful for thinking about the dynamic time-path questions at hand:

Kemp-Wan. The approach of Kemp and Wan (1976) seems to be pertinent to our questions but is not. Evidently, the PTA time-path to $U^\star$ in Figure A.1 can be made monotonic, provided the expanding membership of a PTA always satisfies the Kemp-Wan rule for forming a CU. But what this argument does not say, and indeed cannot say, is that the PTA will necessarily expand in this Kemp-Wan fashion.

Krugman. The same argument applies to the theoretical approach introduced by Krugman (1991), where again the expansion of membership is treated as exogenously specified, as in Viner (1950), and the world welfare consequences of the world's mechanically dividing into a steadily increasing number of symmetric blocs are examined. Srinivasan (1993, 1998) has critiqued the specific conclusions as reversible when symmetry is dropped. But the main problem is the apparent irrelevance of this approach to the incentive-structure dynamic time-path questions that are of central importance today.

"Endogenously Determined" Time-Paths: Recent Theoretical Analyses

The analysis of the dynamic time-path question has moved into formal political economy-theoretic modeling. The following is a synoptic review of the few significant contributions to date, organizing the literature analytically in light of the two questions distinguished above.

Question I. The single contribution that focuses on Question I (i.e., the incentive to add members to a PTA) is by Richard Baldwin (1993), who concentrates on the incentive of nonmembers to join the PTA. He constructs a model to demonstrate that this incentive will be positive: the PTA will create a domino effect, with outsiders wanting to become insiders. The argument is basically driven by the fact that the PTA implies a loss of cost-competitiveness by imperfectly competitive nonmember firms whose profits in the PTA markets decline because they must face the tariffs that member countries' firms do not have to pay. These firms then lobby for entry, tilting the political equilibrium at the margin toward entry demands in their countries. The countries closest to the margin will then enter the bloc, assuming that the members have open entry, thus enlarging the market and thereby increasing the cost of nonmembership and pulling in countries at the next margin. Given the assumptions, including continuity, this domino model can take the PTA time-path to U* in Figure A.1.

Question II. The rest of the theoretical contributions address Question II (i.e., whether the PTA possibility or time-path helps or harms the MTN time-path). Here, the two major analyses to date addressing this question directly and quite aptly, by Krishna (1998) and Philip Levy (1994), reach the "malign-impact" conclusion. Krishna models the political process as the government acting as a "clearinghouse" in response to implicit lobbying by firms. His oligopolistic-competition model shows that the PTA reduces the incentive of the two member countries to liberalize tariffs reciprocally with the nonmember world and that, with sufficient trade diversion, this incentive could be so reduced as to make impossible an initially feasible multilateral trade liberalization. Levy, who models the political process using a median-voter model, works with scale economies and product variety to demonstrate that bilateral FTAs can undermine political support for multilateral free trade. At the same time, a benign impact is impossible in this model: if a multilateral free trade proposal is not feasible under autarky, the same multilateral proposal cannot be rendered feasible under any bilateral FTA. The Krishna and Levy models therefore throw light on the incentive structure questions at hand when the agents are the lobbying groups and interests that are affected by different policy options. However, there are contributions, including that by Kyle Bagwell and Robert Staiger (1993), that take the conventional view of governments as agents maximizing social welfare but then ask whether the effect of allowing PTAs to form affects outcomes concerning trade policy relating to the multilateral system.

   In conclusion, among the unformalized arguments that drive the simultaneous use of PTAs by the United States alongside multilateralism is that produced by Bhagwati (1994) and discussed in chapter 3. He posits a "selfish hegemon" that, though wedded to multilateral outcomes, uses the PTA approach as a sequential bargaining strategy to divide the nonhegemonic governments and improve the final multilateral outcome in favor of its own demands. Koichi Hamada (1995) has analyzed theoretically the differential (static) implications of the classic Charles Kindleberger (1981) "altruistic hegemon" and the Bhagwati (1994) "selfish hegemon" theses.

References

Bagwell, Kyle, and Robert Staiger. 1993. "Multilateral Cooperation During the Formation of Free Trade Areas." Working Paper No. 4364, National Bureau of Economic Research, Cambridge, Mass. (Published in 1997, *International Economic Review*.)

Baldwin, Richard. November 1993. "A Domino Theory of Regionalism." Working Paper No. 857, Centre for Economic Policy

Research, London. (Published in 1995, *Expanding European Regionalism: The EU's New Members.*)

Bhagwati, Jagdish. 1968. "Trade Liberalization among LDCs, Trade Theory and GATT Rules." In J. N. Wolf, ed., *Value, Capital, and Growth.* Oxford: Oxford University Press, 21–43.

———. 1991. *The World Trading System at Risk.* Princeton, N.J.: Princeton University Press.

———. 1993. "Regionalism and Multilateralism: An Overview." In Jaime de Melo and Arvind Panagariya, eds., *New Dimensions in Regional Integration.* Cambridge: Cambridge University Press, 22–51.

———. 1994. "The World Trading System." *Journal of International Affairs* 48, no. 1: 279–85.

Bhagwati, Jagdish, and Arvind Panagariya. 1996. "Preferential Trading Areas and Multilateralism: Strangers, Friends or Foes?" In Jagdish Bhagwati and Arvind Panagariya, eds., *Free Trade Areas or Free Trade? The Economics of Preferential Trading Agreements.* Washington, D.C.: American Enterprise Institute Press.

Bliss, Christopher. 1994. *Economic Theory and Policy for Trading Blocks.* Manchester, U.K.: Manchester University Press.

Brecher, Richard, and Jagdish Bhagwati. 1981. "Foreign Ownership and the Theory of Trade and Welfare." *Journal of Political Economy* 89, no. 3: 497–511.

Cooper, C. A., and B. F. Massell. 1965. "Toward a General Theory of Customs Unions for Developing Countries." *Journal of Political Economy* 73, no. 5: 461–76.

Frankel, Jeffrey, Ernesto Stein, and Shang-Jin Wei. 1995. "Trading Blocs and the Americas: The Natural, the Unnatural, and the Supernatural." *Journal of Development Economics* 47, no. 1: 61–96.

Grossman, Gene, and Elhanan Helpman. 1995. "The Politics of Free Trade Agreements." *American Economic Review* 85, no. 4: 667–90.

Hamada, Koichi. August, 1995. "A Simple Analytic of a Selfish Hegemon." Working Paper No. 174, Iris Center, University of Maryland.

Johnson, Harry. 1965. "An Economic Theory of Protectionism, Tariff Bargaining, and the Formation of Customs Unions." *Journal of Political Economy* 73, no. 3: 256–83.

Kemp, Murray C., and Henry Wan. 1976. "An Elementary Proposition Concerning the Formation of Customs Unions." *Journal of International Economics* 6, no. 1: 95–97.

Kindleberger, Charles. 1981. "Dominance and Leadership in the International Economy." *International Studies Quarterly* 5, no. 2: 242–54.

Krishna, Pravin. 1998. "Regionalism and Multilateralism: A Political Economy Approach." *Quarterly Journal of Economics* 113: 227–51.

Krishna, Pravin, and Jagdish Bhagwati. April 1994. "Necessarily Welfare-Enhancing Customs Unions with Industrialization Constraints." Working paper, Columbia University. (Published in 1997, *Japan and the World Economy*.)

Krugman, Paul. 1991. "The Move to Free Trade Zones." In Federal Reserve Bank of Kansas City, ed., *Policy Implications of Trade and Currency Zones*. Kansas City, Mo.: Federal Reserve Bank of Kansas City, 7–41.

Levy, Philip. 1994. "A Political Economic Analysis of Free Trade Agreements." Economic Growth Center Discussion Paper No. 718, Yale University.

Ohyama, Michihiro. 1972. "Trade and Welfare in General Equilibrium." *Keio Economic Studies* 9, no. 2: 37–73.

Panagariya, Arvind. 1995. "The Free Trade Area of the Americas: Good for Latin America?" Center for International Economics Working Paper No. 12, University of Maryland. (Published in 1996, *World Economy*.)

Panagariya, Arvind, and Ronald Findlay. 1996. "A Political Economy Analysis of Free Trade Areas and Customs Unions." In Robert Feenstra, Douglas Irwin, and Gene Grossman, eds., *The Political Economy of Trade Reform*. Cambridge, Mass.: MIT Press.

Srinivasan, T. N. 1993. "Discussion." In Jaime de Melo and Arvind Panagariya, eds., *New Dimensions in Regional Integration*. Cambridge: Cambridge University Press, 84–89.

———. 1997. "Common External Tariffs of a Customs Union: The Case of Identical Cobb-Douglas Tastes." *Japan and the World Economy* 9, no. 4: 447–65.

Summers, Lawrence. 1991. "Regionalism and the World Trading System." In Federal Reserve Bank of Kansas City, ed., *Policy Implications of Trade and Currency Zones*. Kansas City, Mo: Federal Reserve Bank of Kansas City, 295–301.

Viner, Jacob. 1950. *The Customs Union Issue*. New York: Carnegie Endowment for International Peace.

Wonnacott, Paul, and Mark Lutz. 1989. "Is There a Case for Free Trade Areas?" In Jeffrey Schott, ed., *Free Trade Areas and U.S. Trade Policy*. Washington, D.C.: Institute for International Economics, 59–84.

Glossary

ACRONYMS

AFL-CIO   The American Federation of Labor–Congress of Industrial
Organizations is a voluntary federation of America's unions, representing more than 13 million men and women
nationwide. The AFL-CIO was formed in 1955 by the
merger of the American Federation of Labor and the
Congress of Industrial Organizations. Headquarters are in
Washington, D.C.

APEC   The Asia-Pacific Economic Cooperation was formed in
1989 to discuss the region's economy, investment, cooperation, and trade. The 21 countries that make up its membership also represent over 60% of the world's economy.

CU   Customs unions are composed of a group of countries that
both eliminate tariffs, quotas, and preferences on trade
between member countries and agree to levy the same
tariffs on imports from outside the group. It is basically an
FTA, but has uniform trade policies with countries outside
the union.

CUFTA   The Canada–United States Free Trade Agreement was an
FTA signed by Canada and the United States in 1988 and

was superseded a few years later by the North American Free Trade Agreement, which included Mexico.

FTA Free trade areas are created when two or more countries decide to eliminate tariffs, quotas, and preferences on most (if not all) goods between them. Unlike a customs union, countries in a free trade area do not have the same trade policies with countries outside the FTA.

FTAA The Free Trade Area of the Americas is a proposed FTA that has made little progress and would cover all the nations in the Americas.

FTAAP The Free Trade Area of Asia and Pacific is a proposed FTA for APEC member nations.

GATS The General Agreement on Trade in Services is among the World Trade Organization's most important agreements. The accord, which came into force in January 1995, is the first and only set of multilateral rules covering international trade in services.

GATT The General Agreement on Tariffs and Trade was first signed in 1947. The agreement was designed to provide an international forum that encourages free trade between member states by regulating and reducing tariffs on traded goods and by providing a common mechanism for resolving trade disputes. The GATT was folded into the World Trade Organization, its successor.

GSP The Generalized System of Preferences exempts less-developed member countries of the WTO from most-favored-nation rules, thus allowing them nonreciprocal preferential access to developed countries' economies.

ILO The International Labor Organization is a UN agency that seeks the promotion of social justice and internationally recognized human and labor rights. It was founded in 1919 and is the only surviving major creation of the Treaty of

Versailles, which brought the League of Nations into being. It became the first specialized agency of the UN in 1946. The ILO formulates international labor standards in the form of conventions and recommendations, setting minimum standards of basic labor rights: freedom of association, the right to organize, the right to collective bargaining, abolition of forced labor, equality of opportunity and treatment, and other standards regulating conditions across the entire spectrum of work-related issues.

IMF   The decision to establish the International Monetary Fund was made at a conference held in Bretton Woods, New Hampshire, in July 1944. The IMF came into official existence on December 27, 1945. The IMF is an international organization of 184 member countries. It was established to promote international monetary cooperation, exchange stability, and orderly exchange arrangements; to foster economic growth and high levels of employment; and to provide temporary financial assistance to countries to help ease balance of payments.

MFN   The most-favored-nation principle is embodied in the GATT (and some other trade treaties). It requires every member of the GATT to extend to all other members the lowest tariff that it has in place on a product. Specific exceptions are allowed in the GATT; for example, Article 24 permits members to deny MFN status to nonmembers of free trade agreements and customs unions.

MTN   Multilateral trade negotiations include the Uruguay Round, the last MTN under GATT auspices, and the Doha Round (or Doha Development Agenda), the fist MTN under the WTO.

NAFTA   There are three different NAFTAs: the North American FTA, the New Zealand–Australia FTA, and the

North Atlantic FTA (which was discussed but not implemented). The most famous of these, the North American Free Trade Agreement, took effect on January 1, 1994.

NGO Nongovernmental organizations are private organizations that pursue activities to relieve suffering, promote the interests of the poor, protect the environment, provide basic social services, or undertake community development. In wider usage, the term can be applied to any nonprofit organization that is independent from government.

PTAs Preferential trade agreements give preferential access to certain products from certain nations by reducing tariffs. Today FTAs are the most typical PTAs.

WTO The World Trade Organization is the only global international organization dealing with the rules of trade between nations. The WTO was created by the Uruguay Round negotiations between 1986 and 1994 and was established on January 1, 1995. At its heart are the general trade agreements negotiated and signed by the bulk of the world's trading nations and ratified in their parliaments. As of July 27, 2007, its membership extended to 151 countries. The organization is based in Geneva, Switzerland.

PHRASES AND CONCEPTS

Bretton Woods institutions

The World Bank and its sister organization, the International Monetary Fund, were created at Bretton Woods, New Hampshire, in 1944. Together they are referred to as the Bretton Woods institutions.

Civil society

Civil society refers to the set of institutions, organizations, and behavior situated between the state, the business world, and the family. Specifically, this includes voluntary and non-profit organizations of many different kinds, philanthropic institutions, social and political movements, other forms of social participation and engagement and the values and cultural patterns associated with them. Popularly, and as used in the book, it is used more narrowly to refer to nongovernmental organizations.

Common markets

A common market is a group of countries that not only eliminates tariffs, quotas, and preferences on trade between member countries and agrees to levy the same tariffs on imports from outside the group, but also eliminates internal barriers to trade in factors of production (i.e., labor and capital). It is basically a customs union, with free movement of labor and capital included.

Core labor rights (or standards)

The ILO Declaration of Fundamental Principles and Rights at Work:

- Freedom of association and the effective recognition of the right to collective bargaining.
- Elimination of all forms of forced or compulsory labor.
- Effective abolition of child labor.
- Elimination of discrimination in employment and occupation.

Domestic NGOs

Domestic NGOs are nongovernmental organizations that address primarily domestic issues, such as quality of water, pesticides, and dowry payment. The Center for Science and the Environment in India is an example.

Global NGOs

Global NGOs are nongovernmental organizations that address global issues, including those raised by the activities of international institutions such as the IMF, the WTO, and the World Bank.

Kyoto Protocol

The accord's formal name is United Nations Framework Convention on Climate Change. It was launched at the Earth Summit in 1992 in Rio de Janeiro, Brazil. The Kyoto Protocol, also known as the Kyoto Treaty, is a step forward from the original framework treaty binding emissions targets reductions; its text was adopted at the Kyoto Conference of the Parties to the Climate Treaty in December 1997 in Japan.

Natural trading partners

Countries are sometimes called natural trading partners when they trade more intensively with each other and, alternatively, when they are close geographically. Several economists argue that PTAs among natural trading partners are more likely to be beneficial.

Organization for Economic Cooperation and Development

The Organization for Economic Cooperation and Development groups 30 member countries in a unique forum to discuss, develop, and refine economic and social policies. The OECD grew out of the Organization for European Economic Cooperation (OEEC), which was formed to administer U.S. and Canadian aid under the Marshall Plan for the reconstruction of Europe after World War II. The OECD took over from the OEEC in 1961.

Portfolio capital

Portfolio capital flows relate to investment that provides the investor with a return on equity but without control over the company, a control that is generally not sought either. Short-term capital flows, such as those whose outflow precipitated the Asian financial crisis, are typically composed of portfolio capital.

Reciprocal Trade Agreements Act, 1934

This act was a response to the explosive failure of the U.S. Smoot-Hawley Act. It provided for a reduction in tariff duties by giving President Franklin Delano Roosevelt the authority to negotiate tariff reductions on a bilateral basis in exchange for compensating tariff reductions.

Regionalism

Regionalism is a term used in the GATT and the WTO to refer to all PTAs, even when they are among nations that cannot meaningfully be considered to be part of a "region."

Rules of origin

With PTAs offering preferential tariff treatment to imported products depending on where they come from, "rules of origin" have to be agreed upon to determine the source from which a product originates. We still do not have a unique, agreed-upon rule. Moreover, PTAs are characterized by a multiplicity of arbitrary rules, tailored to lobbying demands.

Smoot-Hawley tariff, 1930

The Smoot-Hawley Act was signed into law on June 17, 1930; it raised U.S. tariffs on over 20,000 imported goods to record levels and is generally blamed for worsening the Great Depression. It caused U.S. exports and imports to fall by more than half, as many countries retaliated with tariffs of their own.

Spaghetti bowl

With proliferating PTAs, one has a worldwide crisscrossing of preferences defined by different rules of origin and different tariff rates on identical products depending on where a product originates. I have christened the resulting chaos a "spaghetti bowl."

Stumbling blocks and building blocks

PTAs may facilitate or detract from multilateral trade liberalization. In the former case they are "building blocks," and in the latter case they are "stumbling blocks" toward multilateral trade liberalization, according to terminology introduced by me in 1991.

Trade Policy Review Mechanism

The Trade Policy Review Mechanism is the WTO program that ensures member nations keep all of their trade policies transparent, requiring members to publish their trade regulations and notify changes in trade policies to the WTO among other policies. All WTO members are reviewed through the TPRM, with the frequency of each country's review varying according to its share of world trade.

U.S. trade representative

The U.S. trade representative is America's principal trade negotiator and the chief trade policy advisor to the president of the United States, with permanent offices at the World Trade Organization in Geneva as well as in Washington, D.C.

World Economic Forum, Davos

The World Economic Forum was founded in 1971 and is known most prominently for holding an annual meeting in Davos, Switzerland, of business leaders, national political leaders, and selected intellectuals and journalists.

Select Bibliography

The Select Bibliography lists principally those articles and books that
I have found useful over the years in the vast literature that has grown
up on the subject and many that I have drawn upon in writing
this short book.

Articles*

Aggarwal, Vinod K. "The Political Economy of a Free Trade Area of the
Asia-Pacific: A U.S. Perspective." In Charles E. Morrison and
Eduardo Pedros, eds., *An APEC Trade Agenda? The Political Economy
of a Free Trade Area of the Asia-Pacific.* Singapore: ISEAS, 2007.

Bhagwati, Jagdish, David Greenaway, and Arvind Panagariya. "Trading
Preferentially: Theory and Policy." *Economic Journal,* July 1998,
1128–48.

Dent, Christopher. "Full Circle? Ideas and Ordeals of Creating a Free
Trade Area of the Asia-Pacific." *Pacific Review* 20, no. 4 (2007), 447–
74.

Evenett, Simon, and Michael Meier. "An Interim Assessment of the
U.S. Trade Policy of 'Competitive Liberalization' " (July 2006; re-
vised February 2007). *World Economy,* forthcoming.

* See references in the appendix for additional articles. For a list of the
leading articles in the postwar literature, classified functionally, see the table of
contents in Jagdish Bhagwati, Pravin Krishna, and Arvind Panagariya, eds.,
Trading Blocs: Alternative Approaches to Analyzing Preferential Trade Agreements
(Cambridge, Mass.: MIT Press, 1999).

Panagariya, Arvind. "The Free Trade Area of the Americas: Good for Latin America?" In Chris Milner, ed., *Developing and Newly Industrializing Countries,* vol. 1. Cheltenham, UK: Edward Elgar, 1998).

Books

Aggarwal, Vinod K., and S. Urata, eds. *Bilateral Trade Arrangements in the Asia-Pacific: Origins, Evolution, and Implications.* New York: Routledge, 2006.

Anderson, Kym, and Richard Blackhurst, eds. *Regional Integration and the Global Trading System.* London: Harvester Wheatsheaf, 1993.

Bhagwati, Jagdish. *Free Trade Today.* Princeton, N.J.: Princeton University Press, 2003.

————. *The World Trading System at Risk.* Princeton, N.J.: Princeton University Press, 1991.

Bhagwati, Jagdish, Pravin Krishna, and Arvind Panagariya, eds. *Trading Blocs: Alternative Approaches to Analyzing Preferential Trade Agreements.* Cambridge, Mass.: MIT Press, 1999.

Bhagwati, Jagdish, Arvind Panagariya, and T. N. Srinivasan. *Lectures on International Trade.* 2nd ed. Cambridge, Mass.: MIT Press, 1998.

Bliss, Christopher, *Economic Theory and Policy for Trading Blocs.* Manchester, UK: University of Manchester Press, 1994.

De Melo, Jaime, and Arvind Panagariya, eds. *New Dimensions in Regional Integration.* Cambridge: Cambridge University Press, 1993.

Dent, Christopher M. *New Free Trade Agreements in Asia-Pacific.* Basingstoke, UK: Palgrave Macmillan, 2006.

Frankel, J. A. *Regional Trading Blocs in the World Economic System.* Washington, D.C.: Institute for International Economics, 1997.

Irwin, Douglas A., Petros C. Mavroidis, and Alan Sykes. *The Genesis of the GATT.* New York: Cambridge University Press, forthcoming, 2008.

Jackson, John H. *World Trade and the Law of GATT.* Indianapolis: Bobbs-Merrill, 1969.

Krishna, Pravin. *Trade Blocs: Economics and Politics.* Cambridge: Cambridge University Press, 2005.

Lawrence, R. Z. *Regionalism, Multilateralism, and Deeper Integration.* Washington, D.C.: Brookings Institution, 1996.

Mathis, John H. *Regional Trade Agreements in the GATT/WTO*. The Hague: T. M. C. Asser Press, 2002.

Meade, James E. *The Theory of Customs Unions*. Amsterdam: North Holland, 1955.

O'Keefe, Thomas A. *Latin American Trade Agreements*. Leiden, The Netherlands: Martinus Nijhoff, 1997.

Panagariya, Arvind. *Regionalism in Trade Policy: Essays on Preferential Trading*. Singapore: World Scientific Press, 1999.

Ravenhill, J. *APEC and the Construction of Asia-Pacific Regionalism*. Cambridge: Cambridge University Press, 2001.

Viner, Jacob. *The Customs Union Issue*. New York: Carnegie Endowment for International Peace, 1950.

WTO Consultative Board to the Director-General Supachai Panitchpakdi. *The Future of the WTO: Addressing Institutional Challenges in the New Millennium*. Geneva: World Trade Organization, 2005.

Surveys

Baldwin, Richard E., and Anthony J. Venables. "Regional Economic Integration." In G. M. Grossman and K. Rogoff, eds., *Handbook of International Economics, Vol. 3*. Amsterdam: Elsevier, 1995.

Panagariya, Arvind. "Preferential Trade Liberalization: The Traditional Theory and New Developments." *Journal of Economic Literature* 38 (June 2000): 287–331.

Index

developing countries and,
41–47, 98
elimination of, 97
embrace of, xv, 36, 81
endogenously determined
time-paths and, 108–10
exchange rate and, 86
exogenously determined
time-paths and, 108
formation of, 89, 91, 104
free trade and, 15–19
as FTAs, 1, 18
growth of, xii, 19
hegemon-centered, 43–47
history of, 15–16
intra-developing-country,
41–43
Lamy on, 12–13
legitimacy of, 28f
lobbying for, 40–41, 40n26, 70,
79–80, 87, 109–10
manufactured items and, 24
membership incentives for, 89,
109–10
motivation for, 45
MTN acceleration by, 39,
86–88, 105
multilateral nondiscriminatory
trade liberalization v., 15
with natural trading partners,
56–57, 58t
1930s decent of, 5–7
nonmember handicap by,
22
objection to, 49–50
pandemic of, 11–14
participation in, 33f
proliferation of, xi–xii, xvii,
1–14, 25, 89, 100

reported to WTO, 11, 11n11,
13f, 28f
rules of origin and, 120
South America willingness
for, 37
specific commodity tariffs and,
61, 61n14
as threat, 11–12
time-path case of, 104–5,
106f, 107
trade diversion/creation from,
50
trade liberalization and, 21
by U.S., 39–40
Princeton University, 17
*Proposals for Expansion of World
Trade and Employment,* 3
protectionism
lobbying and, 38
pursuit of, 11
by Reagan, 38
Robinson on, 7
U.S. countervailing of, 38–39
world trade and, 5–6
PTAs. *See* preferential trade
agreements

quotas, 5

Raby, Geoffrey, 63
Rangel, Charles, *46, 47*
Reagan, Ronald
free trade and, 38n23
protectionism by, 38
VERs by, 38, 38n24
Reciprocal Trade Agreements
Act, 1934, 119
Regionalism, First, 29–31, 119
influence of, 29